Daniel Hannan was educated at Marlborough and Oriel College, Oxford. He worked as a speechwriter for William Hague and Michael Howard. He has been writing for the *Daily Telegraph* since 1996, and also contributes to numerous other publications including the *Wall Street Journal*, *The Times*, the *Washington Examiner*, *The Spectator*, *The Australian*, *The Catholic Herald*, *Die Welt* (Germany) and *Weltwoche* (Switzerland). He is the author of nine books, of which the most recent – *The New Road to Serfdom: A Letter of Warning to America* – is a *New York Times* bestseller. He blogs every day at www.hannan.co.uk, addressing political and cultural issues.

Tom Kremer was born and brought up in Transylvania. He was deported to the concentration camp of Bergen Belsen, escaped to Switzerland and emigrated to Palestine in 1945. He worked in a kibbutz for a number of years and fought in Israel's War of Independence. He read Philosophy at Edinburgh University and studied at the Sorbonne and King's College, London. As a professional inventor, Kremer has created over 250 games and toys that were licensed worldwide. The ideas company he founded in 1969 has become the leader of its field in Europe and is still going strong. The founding of other successful companies followed in Germany, France and the US. He founded Notting Hill Editions in 2011.

Daniel Hannan

–

A DOOMED
MARRIAGE

–

Why Britain Should Leave the EU

–

Foreword and Afterword
by Tom Kremer

Notting Hill Editions

Published in 2016
by Notting Hill Editions Ltd
Widworthy Barton Honiton Devon EX14 9JS

Designed by FLOK Design, Berlin, Germany
Typeset by CB editions, London

Printed and bound
by T. J. International, Padstow, Cornwall

ISBN 978-1-910749-01-2
www.nottinghilleditions.com

Contents

Tom Kremer

FOREWORD
– An Outsider's View –

> This above all: to thine own self be true,
> And it must follow, as the night the day,
> Thou canst not then be false to any man.
> – William Shakespeare, *Hamlet*

M ainstream Britain has, on the whole, sound political instincts and is well disposed towards her European neighbours. The people are, at the same time, somewhat confused, bored and intimidated by the seemingly unending, and largely repetitive, stream of words engulfing the subject. Many admit openly that the complexities involved are beyond them and they would be relieved to leave the final decisions to the government of the day and their 'expert' advisors. For someone like me, who was born and bred on the Continent, who made his home here and has learned over the past sixty years to appreciate what is so unique and so valuable in the British way of life, this state of affairs is deeply disturbing. For although the ultimate decision will have little impact on my own life, it may make all the difference to the lives of my children and even more so to those of my grandchildren. I believe they face a danger of which they are sublimely unaware.

The threat is not an obvious one. It is not posed by the Vikings, the Armada, Napoleonic or German armies intent on invading these shores. It is subtle, insidious and more difficult to counter because it comes from within the country, as well as from the outside. The British people are being asked by their own political leaders to weaken, or even surrender those very rights, decision-making powers, institutions, laws, self-governing habits that alone can guarantee a degree of individual freedom enjoyed by very few other nations in the world.

The British, not unreasonably, consider themselves normal. Seen from the mainland, however, they are eccentric. Driving on the left, jaywalking with gay abandon, hanging on grimly to awkward imperial measures two hundred years after Napoleon introduced a metric system of logical simplicity, communicating in a language virtually devoid of grammar, are some of the more obvious signs of this eccentricity. So are train spotting, the absence of a written constitution, amateur magistrates, the common law, habeas corpus, idiosyncratic sentencing by ancient judges and self-perpetuating, autonomous institutions like Oxford and Cambridge and the BBC that are controlled neither directly by the state nor by private enterprise. Outstanding leaders like Pitt and Churchill are dismissed at the moment of their greatest triumph, defeats and victories are studied in equal measure, people are unnaturally calm in the face of disasters, congenitally unsystematic, seldom prepared, remarkably casual, while an irreverent sense of humour invades each nook and cranny of everyday life. None of this, or anything like it, pertains to the French or the Germans, nor indeed to any other nation in Europe.

The root of the word 'eccentric' literally means 'tending out of, or away from, a centre'. It is the diametric opposite of 'concentric' that is 'tending towards a centre'. This distinction, once fully grasped, goes a long way towards explaining a continental rift that led to profound, and often unfortunate, misunderstandings. A clear demonstration of the 'centrist' tendency is the Brussels administration set up on the French model, in codes written in the French language by the elite French bureaucracy.

In contrast, the British are intrinsically eccentric in every aspect of their communal life. Power is more widely shared throughout society, its sources are diffuse, the centre itself, despite recent Thatcherite and Blairite tendencies, is less than monolithic. The value placed on individual rights and liberties, on the diversity of personal choice, on invention, enterprise and spontaneity, the tolerance of nonconformity and an attitude of irreverence towards external authority, are all hallmarks of an eccentric society.

The political prospects of a Greater Europe will be determined as much by the differences in mindset and culture of its diverse nations as by the common ground they share. Both concentric and eccentric societies operate within political frameworks created by their specific history. The attempt to force an eccentric society, like the British, into an alien, concentric structure, will have devastating consequences. Such an analysis of concentric versus eccentric societies may yield a surprising insight: it is possible that parliamentary democracy having its origins here, on this island, was not just a historical accident, that it had something to do with the inherent attitude of an eccentric people.

Having lived through the war, the last fifty years of almost perfect peace, the rapprochement of erstwhile enemies, the ease of moving and working across Europe, seems still a near miracle to me. A continent at peace with herself, with nations in close economic collaboration, is a magnificent achievement. The threat to what has been achieved lies not in a supposed natural enmity between her diverse people. It lies, as it always has, in an over-ambitious accumulation of concentric political power, be that in Madrid, Paris, Berlin, Moscow or Brussels. What should concern us all is not the establishment of a successful super state, for that will never happen, but a failed drive towards an unattainable ideal, leaving Europe, as always after such failures, in political ruins. There is just a possibility that a European peoples, left to themselves, will eventually evolve their own administrative structures. We must not allow visionary politicians to jeopardise that chance.

There has been much talk recently of the need for Britain to be engaged in Europe. This is plain nonsense.

Since the Middle Ages, she has never been disengaged from the continent. Through trade, war, alliance and coalitions, Britain has always formed an integral part of Europe, both influencing, and influenced by, the powers of the mainland. British and European politics can only be understood within the context of a shared history. We would certainly be looking at quite a different Europe today had Britain not played such a decisive role in Continental affairs since the days of Louis XIV onwards to the end of the Cold War.

What distinguishes Britain's engagement, as against those of other major players, is a consistent, long-term resistance to any emerging concentric power aimed at dominating the entire Continent. Britain may in her time have accumulated an overseas empire but such a consistent support of the smaller countries against central hegemony in Europe can only be explained in terms of a deep, instinctive distrust of overbearing, centralised political structures. In a fast-changing world, Britain has a vital contribution to make in guiding the political destiny of Europe. But she can only do so if she remains true to her eccentric self.

In Daniel Hannan's concisely argued and powerful essay, he addresses the key issues that we need to consider in the forthcoming referendum. Our future will be shaped by the crucial decision this nation is about to make.

– Introduction –

Human beings are change-averse. Behavioural psychologists have written many books trying to work out why we evolved that way. Whatever the explanation, small-c conservatism is written into our genome. In test after test, asked to risk a smaller sum to win a larger one, people make the mathematically irrational choice to hang on to the smaller.

Supporters of the EU are well aware of the phenomenon. They are relying on it to win them the coming referendum. Psephologists have compiled the results of all referendums and plebiscites held in the modern era, and found that more than 60 per cent of them have favoured the status quo.

We are therefore, unsurprisingly, hearing one argument above all others, namely 'Why risk it?' Alright, say supporters of the EU, the Brussels institutions might be remote and expensive. Alright, they might be incapable of reform. They might be contemptuous of public opinion. They might even be corrupt. But how can you be sure that the alternative won't be worse?

As a strategy, it makes sense. Opinion polls show a widespread dislike of the EU. More than that, they show that most people regard membership as 'a bad

1

thing'. But, of course, resenting something isn't quite the same as walking away from it. Most people grumble about their banks; few take the trouble to move their accounts.

Naturally enough, supporters of the EU don't like to discuss sovereignty or democracy or immigration or the cost of membership or the EU's economic decline or Britain's links to other English-speaking countries. They prefer to conjure vague and inchoate fears. Their vagueness is precisely the point. They don't need to show that Britain's trade access to European markets would be prejudiced, or that our security would be jeopardised; they simply have to suggest that such a thing *might be possible*. Thus do they aim to shift the burden of proof: 'How can you be absolutely certain that this or that negative consequence wouldn't follow? Are you sure you want to take the risk?'

Well, to return to the banking metaphor, one thing that would make us shift our accounts is a belief that the bank might fail. And it is in this sense that the renegotiation process has tilted the balance of advantage back toward leaving.

The EU, after all, is not a settled dispensation. It is an evolving dynamic. We can see the direction in which it is evolving, partly because we can infer from its past behaviour, and partly because its leaders keep telling us where they want to go.

For sixty years, the EU has been moving progressively toward political union. The idea of amalgamating

the member states into a larger polity is not a side effect or an optional extra; it is the EU's primary purpose. As Angela Merkel puts it, 'We need a political
union, which means we must gradually cede powers to
Europe and give Europe control.'

After the renegotiation, we know beyond doubt
that the EU will not change its nature. The hope that
Britain might be able to secure a significant repatria-
tion of power, or reassert the sovereignty of Parliament, has been dashed.

Ask yourself one question. If the EU is so resistant
to making concessions when its second-largest economy is about to vote on withdrawal, when will it ever
be amenable to change? If the UK should vote to stay
in, how could it hope to be taken seriously in future?
Having given its assent in a referendum, Britain would
be deemed to have agreed to the EU's declared aim of
drawing all its members into a fiscal, economic, juridi-
cal, diplomatic, political and military merger.

When David Cameron first proposed a renegotiation followed by a referendum, in his Bloomb-
erg speech at the beginning of 2013, he spoke of
securing a different settlement with the EU, involving
significant and, if necessary, unilateral repatriations
of power. Frankly, what he proposed fell well short
of what most Eurosceptics wanted; but he at least ap-
peared to be asking for a relationship based on trade
and co-operation rather than political amalgamation.

One by one, the Prime Minister's declared aims

have been dropped. He had promised to opt out of EU employment laws and social policies; to repatriate control of criminal justice; to curb the European Court; to disapply the Charter of Fundamental Rights; to recover control of who could settle in the UK. But, as the preliminary talks got underway, it became clear that he had changed tack. Instead of asking 'What deal would best suit Britain?' David Cameron was asking 'What can I be absolutely certain of securing, so that I can declare victory?'

To start with such an agenda, and yet still run into difficulties, is quite an achievement. When you're asking for nothing – when you have abandoned the demand for a treaty change, which was the original reason for delaying the referendum – it is truly extraordinary to encounter resistance.

Then again, perhaps we shouldn't have been surprised. We saw how reluctant the EU was to change in 2014, when the palaeo-federalist Jean-Claude Juncker was appointed by 26 votes to 2 despite David Cameron's loud and public opposition. The United Kingdom's demand for something prompts some of the member states into opposing it on principle. Our influence is not zero; it is negative.

There is no further purpose in trying to pretend – if ever there was – that the EU might be reformed from within. We know that a vote to remain will be a vote for the political integration that has been the EU's declared goal all along.

We know something else, too, which was perhaps not so clear until six or seven years ago. The EU's leaders are prepared to pay any price – or, rather, to exact any price from their tax-paying citizens – to keep the project going. The two chief expressions of the European project were the border-free zone known as Schengen, and the single currency. Both turned out to be fair-weather schemes that failed when the storms came. As the migration crisis undermined Schengen, so the debt crisis cruelly exposed the weaknesses in the euro.

Yet the response, in both cases, was the same: to keep political integration going at any cost. If preserving Schengen meant attracting hundreds of thousands or even millions of illegal immigrants into Europe, so be it. If keeping the euro intact meant inflicting poverty and unemployment across the Mediterranean, *tant pis*.

In the space of a few months, the EU's two greatest achievements were wrecked. Two vast and trunkless legs of stone stand in the desert.

Is this really an organisation that Britain wants to belong to? Forever? Because – on this surely all sides can agree – if we vote to remain, we'll never be asked again. We know that, when it comes to referendums, the EU doesn't take 'no' for an answer. If we vote to leave, that won't be an end, but a beginning: new concessions will be put on the table, and some form of associate membership negotiated. But if we vote to stay, that will be that.

Which is why, paradoxically, voting to leave is

closer to the status quo than voting to remain. Imagine that you are sitting on a bus. The bus is heading somewhere you don't want to go, and the driver keeps looking back over his shoulder and shouting out the destination. 'Next stop, tax harmonisation. Then a common defence policy. Then a single judicial space. Then a federal Europe.' If you don't want to end up at that destination, should you remain immobile in your seat, or should you get off the bus?

For what it's worth, several other passengers seem unhappy with their destination. Perhaps, if one person steps onto the pavement, others might follow. Perhaps, in standing up for the rights of nations against the EU bureaucracy, Britain might – not for the first time – be acting in Europe's interest.

I've lost count of how often I've been told that, because I criticise the Brussels system, I am anti-European. In fact, I speak French and Spanish and have lived and worked all over Europe. I believe that European civilisation has made extraordinary contributions to the happiness of mankind: personal freedom, the rule of law, representative government. It is precisely because the EU is so ready to abandon these precepts in pursuit of deeper integration that I oppose it. I oppose it as someone who is Francophile, Germanophile, Italophile, Hellenophile, Turcophile, Hispanophile, Lusophile – but not Europhile if, by Europhile, we mean wanting to shift more powers from elected national governments to Brussels institutions.

The failed renegotiation has proved beyond doubt that the EU cannot be reformed from within. The one thing that might catalyse change is a major member state opting to leave. Not for the first time, the defence of British independence is also a battle for the freedom and democracy of other European peoples.

– The Official History –

I n September 2010, while its twenty-seven constituent states were struggling to cut their national
budgets, the European Parliament allocated £112.5
million to a new museum in Brussels: the House of
European History. MEPs brushed aside criticism of
the cost, insisting that the project was necessary 'to
cultivate the memory of European history and European unification'.

Politicians are often *un*interested in history, but
rarely *dis*interested. Every state has its foundation
myth, every polity its heroic legends. As a rule, the
more insecure the regime, the tighter it clutches at its
approved narrative.

The EU's semi-authorised version of history goes
something like this. Ever since the break-up of Charlemagne's imperium, if not since the fall of Rome, Europe has been weakened by its divisions. A continent
which shared a common cultural and religious heritage
was shattered into a hundred squabbling princedoms.
These statelets wasted their energies on endless wars.

As technology developed, so the account runs, the
states became more powerful and the wars more de-
structive. At some stage in the Early Modern period, a

terrifying new ingredient was introduced: nationalism. No longer were conflicts largely professional affairs, conducted by kings and their hirelings. From now on, whole populations would be dragged – or, worse, would rush enthusiastically – into murderous battles.

Between 1914 and 1945, the approved version continues, nationalism and war reached their climax. Fifty million Europeans died in the continent's last two great 'civil wars'. At which point, the survivors decided they had had enough. Since nation-states were the cause of war, their dissolution would be the means to peace. France and Germany had been fighting each other on-and-off ever since they came into being at the dissolution of the Carolingian empire in 843. If they were merged again, the problem would be solved. Charles de Gaulle was later to describe the process of European integration as 'a revival of the whole concept of Charlemagne'.[1]

At this moment, the story goes, some visionary Europeans stepped forward. They were not soldiers or statesmen of the old school. Europe had had enough of that. Some were elected politicians, others technocrats. All, though, saw their mandate as coming from their understanding of what needed to be done. There is no formal list of Europe's founding fathers, but seven men are recognised in almost every tally: Konrad Adenauer, Jean Monnet, Paul-Henri Spaak, Alcide

1 *Mémoires d'Espoir: Le Renouveau*, 1970.

De Gasperi, Robert Schuman, Joseph Bech and Johan Willem Beyen.

These men had something in common which is rarely, if ever, remarked. All except Jean Monnet (who was from Cognac) came from the Carolingian heartland. Spaak, Bech and Beyen were, respectively, from the three Benelux states. The Italian, Alcide De Gasperi, was from the Tyrol, which was Austrian at the time of his birth. The German, Konrad Adenauer, was from Cologne close to Charlemagne's capital at Aachen. The Frenchman, Robert Schuman, the man now hailed as the father of the EU, was from Lorraine, which was part of Germany when he was born; his mother was Luxembourgish.

These patriarchs, runs Europe's official history, transcended nationalism, and united Europe in peace. The pooling of Europe's resources made war impractical, and the pooling of sovereignty made it unthinkable.

As Europeans fell into the habit of working together, it became hard to imagine that they would ever again vote for extremists or chauvinists. The European model proved attractive: three more countries joined in 1973, a further three by 1986, three more in 1995, ten in 2004 and two in 2007.

Europe spread its values, according to its apologists, not with bombs, but with trade accords. Its greatest threat to a neighbouring country was not to invade it, but to ignore it. The prospect of European co-operation encouraged applicant nations to adopt more liberal domestic policies. Poland softened its abortion laws, Croatia handed over its war-criminals, Turkey eased restrictions on its minorities.

More and more countries opted voluntarily to belong. Europe's mixed market model – neither so harsh as American capitalism nor so authoritarian as Soviet communism – proved irresistible. Other parts of the world began to form themselves into regional blocs in mimicry of the EU: ASEAN, Mercosur, the African Union and so on. These associations were, indeed, initially sponsored by Brussels, which continues to bolster them by refusing to sign trade or aid accords with individual states, instead insisting on 'bloc-to-bloc' deals.

As more and more countries are drawn into the Eurosphere, the tale concludes, and as aggressive patriotism recedes across the world, we are approaching something like the end of history. At any rate, the nationalist demons that have tormented humanity through the centuries are at last being exorcised.

That, as I say, is the official version and, like all official versions, it contains specks of truth. Certainly, its core element – the belief that European integration is an antidote to nationalism and war – is sincerely believed by most supporters of the project.

Nonetheless, every aspect of this narrative needs qualification, starting with the premise that the breakup of empires into smaller units is bad for progress. All the evidence suggests that the opposite is true.

Europe's rise to global hegemony came at a time when, unlike the great civilisations of Asia, it was politically disunited. Five hundred years ago, the Oriental dynasties – the Mings in China, the Moguls in India, the Ottomans in the Near and Middle East – held a clear technological lead over the scattered peoples at the Western tip of the Eurasian landmass. European visitors to the Eastern courts marvelled at what they saw: gunpowder, paper money, canals, advanced mathematics, medicine, astronomy and cartography. It would have seemed a safe bet that the Asian powers would dominate Europe for the rest of the Millennium, that the Chinese would sail around Africa to plant trade missions in Portugal rather than the other way around.

In fact, Europe's disunity turned out to be its strength. The Oriental monarchies, being unitary states, became uniform, regulated and highly taxed. Innovation was stifled, and bureaucracy burgeoned. But Europe never became a single state. Instead, its constituent entities jostled and strove to outdo each other. New ideas could be tried in one place and, if successful, copied in others. As Paul Kennedy showed in *The Rise and Fall of the Great Powers*, such diversity encouraged enterprise and risk-taking.[2] Just as competition among individuals tends to boost growth, so does competition among states.

2 Kennedy popularised the theory, but acknowledged that it was first proposed by the Australian historian E. L. Jones in his 1987 study, *The European Miracle*.

One of the saddest aspects of European integration is that the current EU mandarinate – the appellation is unusually apposite in this context – is determined to go down the Ming-Mogul-Ottoman route to harmonisation at the very moment that the great nations of Asia have discovered the virtues of devolution and decentralisation.

In the name of Europe, Eurocrats have undone the secret of Europe's success: the diversity, variety and pluralism that raised their continent to greatness.

There were some critics who saw this clearly at the outset. The renowned liberal economist Wilhelm Röpke, who had been one of the first Germans to apprehend the Nazi menace, grasped right away that the ambitions of the Euro-patriarchs would jeopardise Europe's cultural success. In 1960, as France, Germany and the Benelux states made their first tentative steps toward integration, he made a perceptive observation:

In antiquity, Strabo spoke of the 'many shapes' of Europe; Montesquieu would speak of Europe as a 'nation de nations'; in our own time Christopher Dawson has stressed Europe's character of a 'society of peoples.' Decentrism is of the essence of the spirit of Europe. To try to organise Europe centrally, to subject the Continent to a bureaucracy of economic planning, to weld it into a bloc, would be nothing less than a betrayal of Europe and the European patrimony. The betrayal would be the more perfidious for being perpetrated in the name of Europe and by an outrageous misuse of that name.

– *A Humane Economy* (1960)

The notion that size is a precondition of prosperity is belied by the facts. If it were true, China would be wealthier than Hong Kong, Indonesia than Brunei – the EU itself, for that matter, would be wealthier than Switzerland. All the evidence suggests that the opposite is the case: that states flourish economically when decisions are taken as closely as possible to the people they affect.

The tables below show where the wealthiest people in the world live according, respectively, to the IMF and the World Bank.

1	Qatar	137,162
2	Luxembourg	97,639
3	Singapore	83,066
4	Brunei	79,890
5	Kuwait	70,686
6	Norway	67,166
7	United Arab Emirates	66,347
8	San Marino	60,887
9	Switzerland	58,149
10	Hong Kong	55,097

International Monetary Fund 2014

1	Qatar	146,178	2014
2	Macau	139,767	2014
3	Luxembourg	91,048	2013
4	Singapore	82,763	2014
5	Kuwait	76,886	2013
6	Brunei	75,699	2014
7	Norway	64,893	2014
8	United Arab Emirates	63,497	2014
9	Switzerland	56,939	2013
10	Hong Kong	55,084	2014

World Bank 2011–2014

All these polities are tiny. The most populous among them is Switzerland, with just over eight million inhabitants. And Switzerland is the most decentralised state on Earth, governing itself like a confederation of statelets. Swiss cantons decide, not only their own tax, welfare and social policies; but even, to a degree, their residence and migration policies.

Almost as devolved as Switzerland is the state that just misses both lists, coming eleventh according to both the IMF and the World Bank, namely the United States. The United States is the exception that proves the rule: a country with a large population that none the less has wealthy citizens. Its wealth rests on the juris-dictional competition that comes from massive internal autonomy. In some senses, the fifty states of the US enjoy more sovereignty than nations within the EU, on issues ranging from indirect taxation to capital punishment.

A country's wealth is not determined by the size of its territory or population, but by the policies it pursues. If anything, as a glance at Europe tells us, it is far better to live in small, non-EU states such as Iceland, Norway and Switzerland, than in the blundering behemoth that the EU has become.

What, though, of the contention that political unity secures peace and freedom? This, for most Euro-integrationists, was the greater consideration. Their speeches and writings were focused on the political, rather than the economic, virtues of amalgamation. Though they didn't care to say so, they were prepared to risk a decline in economic growth as the price for unity. War, they liked to tell anyone who listened, was far more deleterious to wealth creation than anything else.

Again, the notion that large political units are more peaceful or more liberal than small ones is easier to uphold in theory than in practice.

Stability, though an end in itself for many diplomats, is an overrated virtue. A tyranny can be a remarkably stable entity; and while stability is generally in the interests of the tyrant, it is rarely in the interest of his subjects. The Soviet Union was the largest multinational state of modern times and, though it was certainly stable, it was a wretched place to live.

To this day, Euro-diplomats tend to place great

emphasis on constancy; more so, in many instances, than on freedom. Think of the international questions on which the US and EU diplomatic machines fundamentally differ – whether to deal with the anti-Castro resistance in Cuba, whether to engage with the ayatollahs in Tehran, whether to back Taiwan – and you will descry a pattern. The Brussels official is keener than his State Department counterpart to work with what he finds, to deal with existing rulers, to encourage reform rather than seek regime change. The European Union, born out of a reaction against disunity and war, favours stability over democracy. The United States, born out of a popular revolt against a remote regime, reverses those priorities.

Stability, almost by definition, suits the people in charge. It is therefore the justification of every dictatorship: *après moi, le deluge.* Such a plea is perhaps likelier to resonate with the Euro-functionary, himself the product of an essentially undemocratic system, than with an elected representative.

Yet there is no intrinsic virtue in a large, stable state – especially when its size and stability are purchased at the expense of freedom.

This point was beautifully made by Edward Gibbon, a Europhile by almost any contemporary standard, and a nostalgist for the Roman Empire whose collapse he chronicled. Gibbon saw advantages in political unity, and argued that the best moment in human history to have been alive was the second century AD, between the death of the Emperor Domitian and the accession of the Emperor Commodus. Yet he also recognised that the advantages of peace and stability were outweighed by the dangers inherent in pan-continental rule:

The division of Europe into a number of independent states, connected, however, with each other by the general resemblance of religion, language, and manners, is productive of the most beneficial consequences to the liberty of mankind. A modern tyrant, who should find no resistance either in his own breast, or in his people, would soon experience a gentle restraint from the example of his equals, the dread of present censure, the advice of his allies and the apprehension of his enemies. The object of his displeasure, escaping from the narrow limits of his dominions, would easily obtain, in a happier climate, a secure refuge, a new fortune adequate to his merit, the freedom of complaint and, perhaps, the means of revenge.

— *The History of the Decline and Fall of the Roman Empire*, 1776

Gibbon was well aware of the vital importance of political asylum. He understood that driving people into exile tended to debilitate the tyranny from which they were banished and strengthen the land that received them. To pluck one example from the many with which he was familiar, France had expelled her Protestant population with the Revocation of the Edict of Nantes in 1685. At a stroke, Louis XIV lost 400,000 of his most enterprising subjects. The refugees fled to Great Britain, Switzerland, North America, South Africa and the Low Countries and, in so doing, tipped the balance of power permanently and comprehensively against the power that had ejected them.

Britain was in a state of intermittent conflict with France between 1689 and 1815. On paper, France had all the advantages: a greater territory, richer resources and a population nearly four times the size of her rival's. Yet Britain emerged ultimately victorious because she made up in enterprise what she lacked in territorial advantages. In particular, she developed modern capital markets, allowing her to concentrate resources in a way that the French never could. That process owed a great deal to the Huguenot exiles, whose energy would otherwise have been placed at the disposal of the Bourbons.

The phenomenon of the enterprising asylum-seeker has been observed many times since, the outstanding example perhaps being the intellectual contribution made to the Allied cause by Jews who had been forced to flee fascist Europe.

Which brings us neatly to the single greatest dissonance in the EU-approved version of history, namely the conviction that European integration was and is an antidote to the horrors of Nazism.

From the beginning, this has been the backstop of every integrationist argument. Alright, the Common Agricultural Policy (CAP) might be wasteful, but surely it's a small price worth paying for peace! True, the budget might not have been approved for eighteen years, but at least there are no more fascist demagogues! You don't like the lack of democracy in Brussels? Would you rather have a second Holocaust?

This last argument was made quite blatantly by the then Swedish Commissioner, Margot Wallström, in the run-up to the French and Dutch plebiscites on the European Constitution in 2005. Attending a ceremony to mark the anniversary of the liberation of the Terezin ghetto in the Czech Republic, she warned that 'No' votes in the coming referendums might lead to another genocide:

There are those today who want to scrap the supra-national idea. They want the EU to go back to the old purely inter-governmental way of doing things. I say those people should come to Terezin and see where that old road leads.[3]

– *Sunday Telegraph*, 15 May 2005

There are several objections to be made to this thesis (beyond the obvious one that it turned out to be false: France and the Netherlands both voted 'No', yet there has been no Nazi revival).

Most strikingly, any ideology that presents itself as the sole alternative to fascism is allowing itself a great deal of leeway. After all, if European integration were

3 The Commissioner doctored her website to remove the offending words after they were publicised by this author.

the only thing that stood in the way of war and genocide, it could get away with being remarkably illiberal and undemocratic while yet remaining the better option.

I don't make this point glibly. In the seventeen years I have spent as an MEP, I have heard the excuse trotted out again and again. When a Euro-federalist is confronted with some monstrous failing of the Brussels system, one which he feels unable to justify, he will almost invariably say: 'OK, OK, but at least it's better than nationalism'.

It's not a new tactic. The Stalinist regimes of the Council for Mutual Economic Assistance (Comecon) states initially called themselves Anti-Fascist Fronts. Their leaders, like many contemporary Eurocrats, half-believed their own propaganda. In their own eyes, at least, they had earned some sort of mandate through their active resistance to Hitler. While others had collaborated, they, the small cadre of Communists, had been imprisoned for their beliefs, or had waged partisan guerrilla campaigns. The conviction that Communism was the practical alternative to fascism formed the basis, in private at any rate, of their sense of legitimacy. In Czechoslovakia, Yugoslavia and the GDR, at least in the early days, it was also a public justification.

As an aside, it is interesting to note that, despite their later adoption of the anti-Nazi cause, few of the early Euro-leaders had had especially glorious war records. A handful, notably the Italian Christian Democrat, Alcide de Gasperi, had actively opposed fascism.

A few more, such as François Mitterand, had actively collaborated. Most had simply kept their heads down.

In his seminal study *The Tainted Source*, John Laughland showed that the Euro-patriarchs had been keener than the population at large on working with fascist and Quisling regimes.[4]

Of course, those who have never had to live through a military occupation should not rush to judgment. There is no suggestion that the anti-fascism of the Euro-patriarchs was insincere. On the contrary, they were plainly genuine in their conviction that they were burying the horrors through which they had recently passed.

Harder to shake off, perhaps, is the way in which the 'Europeanist' propaganda employed by the Nazis and their allies continued into the 1950s, albeit in an adjusted and democratic form. Both at an intellectual and a popular level, fascist regimes in the early 1940s had justified themselves by positing a European identity. Europe, they argued, was a haven of civilization between two forms of barbarism: the Anglo-Saxon savagery of unregulated markets and crass commercialism, and the Soviet savagery of total communism. That argument has never entirely gone away.

Ideas are not responsible, of course, for the people who take them up. I mention this coincidence of imagery simply to contextualise the assertion that European

4 *The Tainted Source: The Undemocratic Origins of the European Idea*, 1997.

integration is an antidote to Nazism. Before making a claim of such magnitude, Euro-enthusiasts should be absolutely certain of their moral right to do so.

To repeat, modern Europhiles are unquestionably sincere in their dislike of Nazism. Nothing is more misplaced than the suggestion, which one occasionally hears all over Europe that the EU is really some sort of continuation of German expansionism. Quite apart from being terrifically rude, the charge is the opposite of the truth. Far from harbouring secret imperial ambitions, most modern Germans suffer from a lack of patriotism that borders almost on self-abnegation.

The reason that John Laughland's work is worth citing is that, having made such an issue out of their anti-Nazi credentials, supporters of the European project invite an evaluation of that argument. I'd much rather not be discussing the issue at all – references to the Second World War in modern politics should be entered into, as the Prayer Book says of matrimony, reverently, discreetly, advisedly, soberly. But, by constantly arguing that the EU is the only reason we have enjoyed peace since 1945, the integrationists more or less oblige us to address the question. Here, for example is Herman van Rompuy:

We have together to fight the danger of a new Euroscepticism. The biggest enemy of Europe today is fear. Fear leads to egoism, egoism leads to nationalism, and nationalism leads to war.
    – Speech in Berlin, 9 November 2010

Here is Angela Merkel:

Nobody should believe that another half century of peace in Europe is a given – it's not. So I say again: if the euro collapses, Europe collapses. That can't happen.
– Speech to the Bundestag, 24 October 2011

Alright, then. Since we have been forced into this distasteful debate, let's at least be accurate. Was the EU a *cause* of European peace, or was it a *consequence* of the peace brought about by the defeat of fascism, the spread of democracy and the Nato alliance? Is it a vaccine against Nazism, or simply the latest in a long line of presumptuous supra-national ideologies?

The notion that, as Herman Van Rompuy puts it, 'nationalism leads to war' is more often asserted than explained. Looking back over the past half millennium, we find plenty of wars that have ideological rather than national roots. Europe was, for example, more often plunged into conflict by religious rather than by national differences. The wars of the Counter-Reformation were not patriotic conflicts. From Münster to Drogheda, terrible atrocities were committed by men of the same blood and speech. The Thirty Years War (1618-1648) was the longest continuous war in Europe's history and, on some measures, proportionately the most lethal, yet it divided people by faith, not nationality. As the ever-wise historian Lord Macaulay wryly observed:

The experience of many ages teaches us that men may be ready to fight to the death, and to persecute without pity, for a religion whose creed they do not understand, and whose precepts they habitually disobey.

– *The History of England from the Accession of James the Second*, 1848

More recently, political differences came to replace religious ones, generating the same fanaticism in twentieth century men that sectarianism had been capable of generating in their great-grandparents. Fascism and Communism were to cause far more death and destruction than any nationalist conflicts. It's true, of course, that, as with any wars, national interests became entangled with the doctrinal schisms. The Second World War and the Cold War were not simply ideological clashes; they also ranged whole countries against each other. But they were *primarily* ideological wars, which cut across national differences.

This was obviously true of the Cold War, but it was true, too, of the Nazi aggression. There wasn't a country in Europe which didn't have combatants on both sides. When Berlin fell in 1945, the last troops still standing in its defence were the Scandinavian and French soldiers of, respectively, the Nordica and Charlemagne Waffen-SS regiments (both of which, incidentally, had sought recruits on grounds of 'defending Europe').[5]

5 Antony Beevor, *Berlin: The Downfall 1945*, 2002.

Where nationalism *was* at the root of a conflict, it was usually nationalism of a people who had been, as it were, incorporated into the wrong state. The nineteenth century saw several wars which began as risings against foreign rule, or as attempts to embrace *irredenti* populations. When Euro-enthusiasts blame the two world wars on 'nationalism', they rarely emphasise what *kind* of nationalism it was. The Great War was sparked by the demand of the South Slav citizens of Austria-Hungary for statehood; the Second World War by Hitler's annexation of German-speaking parts of Poland. It's true, of course, that these were by no means the only causes of their respective conflagrations. Still, the point is worth emphasising. Look around the world today, and see how many conflicts are rooted in the misalignment of state borders with national affinities. It is hard to find much basis for the contention that jamming different nationalities together makes them less rather than more antagonistic.

As for the Wallström/Terezin line of reasoning, if we absolutely must drag the Holocaust into the argument, it is worth stressing that national citizenship was, for many European Jews and other victims, their only defence against the murderers. In his chilling, matter-of-fact chronicle of the killings, Robert Wistricht noted that even fascist and collaborationist regimes tended to draw a distinction between their own nationals and refugees who had fled to their territory. Most Axis and occupied governments recognised an obligation to their Jewish citizens which (with the exception of Denmark and the partial exception of Bulgaria) they refused to extend to foreign nationals who had entered their jurisdiction as the result of persecution elsewhere. The Nazis well understood this tendency, which was why one of their first acts, on seizing control of a new territory, was to declare all Jews stateless.[6]

The worst massacres took place in those parts of Europe where there was nothing resembling a national government, namely the Nazi-occupied parts of Poland, Lithuania and the USSR. The Jewish inhabitants of these territories were statistically far less likely to survive the war than those in the Third Reich itself.

In his 2015 study, *Black Earth*, Professor Timothy Snyder of Yale University explained why. Statehood and sovereignty ensured a measure of due process. A German who sheltered a Jewish family might face trial and incarceration; a Pole who did the same would have his own family summarily murdered before his eyes.

Professor Snyder observes that Hitler disliked and aimed to dismantle the institutions of the nation-state. The result was catastrophic for vulnerable groups:

The likelihood that Jews would be sent to their deaths depended upon the durability of institutions of state sovereignty and the continuity of prewar citizenship. These structures created the matrix within which individual choices were

6 Robert Wistricht, *Hitler and the Holocaust*, 2001.

made, the constraints upon those who did evil, and the possi-
bilities for those who wished to do good.

Those who did the most good in Holocaust Europe were precisely those who could offer access to the
rights of citizenship. Ho Feng-Shan, the Chinese consul
in Vienna, issued at least 1,000 visas good for travel to
Shanghai after the Anschluss of 1938. In the summer of
1940, Chiune Sugihara, the Japanese consul in Soviet-
occupied Lithuania, saved some 8,000 lives (two-thirds
of them Jewish) by issuing travel visas that allowed the
bearers to traverse the Soviet Union and exit for the
Dutch island of Curaçao. After the fall of Paris in 1940,
the Spanish and Portuguese consuls in Bordeaux issued many thousands of visas to fleeing French Jews.
Most famously, Raoul Wallenberg issued Swedish passports to Hungarian Jews and offered them sanctuary
within Swedish embassy buildings. The Nazis did not
respect much, but they respected paperwork.

I make this point, not simply for the sake of challenging Mrs Wallström's interpretation of history, but
to draw attention to the role of the nation-state as a
defender of liberty. Over the years, national units have
proved remarkably secure vessels of freedom. One
after another, various 'isms' have arisen which purport
to be bigger than the nation-state. In each case, their
very presumption, their refusal to recognise accepted
notions of state sovereignty or territorial jurisdiction,
makes them volatile. And, in each case, nation-states,

rooted as they are in genuine affinities, have been bulwarks against them.

In the twentieth century, two monstrous ideologies claimed to transcend national jurisdiction: fascism and communism. In our own age, similar claims are made by Islamic fundamentalism.

The Iranian Revolution, like the French and the Russian, regarded itself as bigger than the nation-state. Its signature act was the siege of the US embassy: a shocking violation of all accepted norms of international law. Even during the Second World War, when mutually opposed ideologies strove to extirpate each other, diplomats were peaceably evacuated through neutral states. In signalling their disregard for national sovereignty, the ayatollahs were announcing that their legitimacy came from a source higher than the recognised law of nations. That is always a dangerous conceit and, like the Bolsheviks before them, they immediately sought to replicate their revolution around the world, sponsoring militias from the Balkans to Central Asia, striking as far afield as London and Buenos Aires.

The nation-state, with all its imperfections, was and is a rampart against ideologies which spill out violently from behind borders. Precisely because nation-states have grown organically, and are rooted in a degree of popular consent, they have a natural bias against belligerent and revolutionary doctrines. The idea that nationalism is an unstable or dangerous force is, indeed, a remarkably new one.

During the Second World War, a constant theme of Churchill's rhetoric, and of Allied propaganda more generally, was that Britain was fighting for the cause of all nations. Patriotism was not simply the focus of Britain's resistance to tyranny; it extended also to a respect for the freedom of friendly peoples. Britain had declared war in the first place in 1939 (as it had in 1914) because of the violation of the sovereignty of another country. Again and again, in their war aims and in their broadcasts to occupied Europe, the Allies stressed that they were fighting to restore the independence of nation-states throughout Europe.

This difference in perception partly explains why the United Kingdom was reluctant to involve itself in the first moves towards European federalism in the 1950s. British people did not share the sense that the nation-state had failed, or that patriotism was dangerous. They understood, from their recent experience that, far from denigrating other countries, a genuine patriot values the freedom of all peoples.

As the Second World War recedes from memory, Europeans can take a more measured view of national loyalties. The reflexive equation of nationalism with chauvinism and war, which predominated in the 1950s, can now be placed in context. It is time, in short, to examine the case for the nation-state.

2

– The Case for Nationalism –

When a *bien pensant* Europhile wishes to signal his strongest possible disapproval of something, he will use one of two words: 'nationalist' or 'populist'. Both epithets have become somewhat detached from their literal definitions. To adapt George Orwell on the word 'fascist', they have now little meaning except in so far as they signify 'something not desirable'.[1]

It is nonetheless interesting to see the two words so often yoked together, for they both carry a democratic implication. Any referendum that results in a rejection of closer European integration (which is to say, almost every referendum on the subject) is dismissed as both nationalist and populist. Any politician who accepts the result of such a poll is given both soubriquets in an especially bellicose tone.

They are indeed linked concepts. As Charles de Gaulle put it in 1942:

La démocratie se confond exactement, pour moi, avec la souveraineté nationale. La démocratie c'est le gouvernement du

1 *Politics and the English Language*, 1946.

peuple par le peuple, et la nationale, c'est le peuple exerçant sa souveraineté sans entrave.

    – Press conference in London, 25 May 1942

Nowadays, that notion sounds a little archaic; but in 1942, it would have seemed obvious. Democracy in its modern form had always been linked to the national principle. When radicals in the eighteenth and nineteenth centuries began to argue for one-man-one-vote, they almost invariably found themselves challenging the existing multi-national units that existed across Europe. Having posited the revolutionary idea that government should be carried out by and for the people, they found that they had immediately raised another question: what people? Within what unit, in other words, were these democratic arguments to be played out?

That question had only one possible answer, and the democrats found it at once. Representative government, they argued, would work best within a population whose members felt enough in common one with another to accept government from each other's hands: in other words, within a nation. As the Italian patriot Giuseppe Mazzini put it, in perhaps the pithiest ever statement of the case for self-determination: 'Where there is a nation, let there be a state'.

A community of identity might rest on many things: history, geography, culture or religion. Language is the most common basis for nationhood, but there are exceptions. A strong sense of national identity can exist in a multi-lingual territory (Switzerland, for example); conversely, a monolingual population might contain more than one national identity (as among the Serbo-Croat speakers of the former Yugoslavia).

It is important to stress that these things are rarely straightforward. People are capable of sustaining more than one identity: you might feel Scottish as well as British, Corsican as well as French. Identities can mutate over time. An arbitrary political frontier might, as the decades pass, become a genuine national one (something of the sort has happened between Austria and Southern Germany, and across much of South America). And, of course, languages themselves are political. When, following devolution, Irish was recognized as an official language in Northern Ireland (despite not being the native tongue of anyone born there), Unionists responded by granting equal status to 'Ulster Scots' – which until then had been generally considered a patois. As the Yiddish linguist Max Weinreich observed, 'a language is a dialect with an army and navy'.[2]

None of these complications, though, compromises the essential principle. A polity functions best when there is a sense of shared identity. That sense, being visceral, might defy logical definition; but it is no less real for that.

2 'A shprakh iz a dialekt mit an armey un flot', YIVO Bleter, 1945.

Multi-national democracies are rarely stable. By multi-national, I don't mean a society which is in the process of assimilating minorities, nor yet one with small foreign populations. Virtually every state in the world has some minorities, if only as the result of immigration. I am talking here of states where large and settled communities have different loyalties. Many such states have existed through history, but they have rarely been democratic. Indeed, the rule is that, once their peoples are given the vote, they opt for separation. The Soviet and Yugoslav federations went the same way as the Ottoman and Habsburg empires: their constituent peoples couldn't be held together once they were free to choose.

To repeat, these things are rarely clear-cut. A multi-national democracy can unravel slowly and peacefully, as Belgium has been doing for decades. It can tolerate a measure of continuing secessionist discontent without ceasing to be democratic, as India does.

And, of course, not all separatist feelings are of equal intensity. To take two examples, one from either end of the spectrum, the world's newest state, South Sudan, was different in almost every way from the rest of Sudan: ethnically, religiously, linguistically. It had been through a secessionist war, and eventually broke away in rancour and enmity. No one, by contrast, has ever fired a shot in anger over the issue of Scottish secession. Indeed, it is far from clear that Scottish identity is of the kind that generally constitutes national separateness. On most of the usual denominators, Scotland forms part of the same national continuum as the rest of the United Kingdom. Scots watch the same television programmes, follow the same sports, eat the same food, shop at the same chains and speak the same language as people elsewhere in Britain. As the aboriginal Unionist, James VI & I put it:

Hath not God first united these Kingdoms, both in Language and in Religion and in Similitude of Manners? Yea, hath He not made us all in one Island, compassed by one Sea, and of itself by Nature so indivisible, as almost those that were Borderers themselves on the late Borders, cannot distinguish nor know or discern their own limits?
– Accession speech to Parliament, 1603

Sure enough, when the referendum came in September 2014, pro-independence campaigners could not rely, as their South Sudanese equivalents could, on an obvious sense of national difference. Instead, they had to base their arguments around more practical assertions: independence would boost growth, independence would mean scrapping Trident, independence would mean no more Tory governments. When polling day came, campaigners on both sides put out their flags: the saltire for Yes campaigners, the Union flag for No. Some Scots felt attachment only to the first; most, the result suggests, recognised a dual identity and, by 55 to 45 per cent, Scotland voted to remain part of the British nation. In South Sudan, by contrast, people were in no doubt that they formed a separate race, and voted by 98 per cent in a referendum for secession.

For all these shades of grey, the principle holds. Other things being equal, our inclination should be to allow people to determine their own borders. Or, to put it another way, the most important consideration when determining national frontiers should be the wishes of the inhabitants. This is not to say that alternative claims – geography, history, past treaties, rights of the residual state to access – have no force; simply that they ought not to override the claim of self-determination.

This point is worth emphasising because, at present, our ruling ideology is based on precisely the opposite principle. International organisations – naturally enough, you might say – actively *oppose* the national principle. The UN and the EU, in particular, hold up the multi-national state as a desirable end in it-self, and are prepared to invest considerable resources in ensuring that state borders don't coincide with ethnographic ones.

This is most obvious in the case of the two European territories that the international community administers as protectorates: Bosnia-Herzegovina and Kosovo. The former is run by an EU-appointed High Representative, the latter by a UN-approved general. In both cases, the primary purpose of such rule is to prevent a readjustment of borders along the lines that local people favour.

In neither case is the territorial integrity of the state based on a fear of ethnic cleansing. On the contrary, the Serbs of both territories are now clustered conveniently close to Serbia proper. In the case of Kosovo, the *de facto* border is already the ethnographic one. But to regularise this line would mean accepting the validity of national self-determination as a concept – which would, of course, destroy the intellectual foundations of the entire European project. As Upton Sinclair used to observe, it is remarkably difficult to make a man understand something when his salary depends upon his not understanding it.

And so, in pursuit of multi-nationalism, democracy is vitiated. Dozens of elected officials have been dismissed in Bosnia-Herzegovina for, in effect, failing to uphold the EU's approved orthodoxy of multi-nationalism. Both states have adopted variants of the EU flag – stars on a blue background – so as to emphasize their post-national nature. Kosovo's first national anthem was the EU's own Ode to Joy. When it eventually wrote its own, it plumped for a wordless tune called 'Europe'.

In other words, the EU is exporting its ideology, just as it does when seeking to force non-European states into their own regional unions. It is determined to ensure that neighbouring countries form political units based on something other than the national principle. Why? Because European construction itself rests on the doctrine that national loyalties are arbitrary, transient and discreditable. When it bars the election of nationalist politicians in its satrapies, it is simply extending the principle that leads it to disallow 'no' votes in referendums within its own borders. De Gaulle was right to say that democracy and national self-determination are the same thing. Deny the second and, pretty soon, you find yourself having to deny the first.

While on the subject of the Balkans, it's worth dealing with one of the more common objections to the right of self-determination, namely the idea that partition is invariably a wretched and violent experience. It can be, of course. Any change in political borders is potentially disruptive. In British India, partition resulted in terror and bloodshed, and in repeated wars between India and Pakistan. In Ireland (or, strictly speaking, in the United Kingdom, which was the entity partitioned in 1921), there were civil wars on both sides of the new frontier: a short and intense one to the south, a protracted and intermittent one to the north.

In both cases, though, it can at least be argued that these problems were greatly exacerbated by a failure properly to apply the national principle. The treaty which established Northern Ireland also provided for a Boundary Commission to redraw the border. It met between 1922 and 1925 and duly recommended substantial changes: the Irish Free State would have gained most of South Armagh and Co Londonderry, and ceded a chunk of Co Donegal, along with some other minor adjustments. Had these alterations been implemented, much subsequent anguish might have been averted.

In India, the failure was even greater: more Muslims were stranded in India than incorporated into Pakistan, and parts of the border bore no relation whatever to local preferences. These regions – above all, Kashmir, whose promised plebiscite was never held – have been in a state of semi-permanent conflict ever since, serving to poison relations between Pakistan and India.

In any case, it is misleading to hold up the worst cases as typical. There are plenty of examples of peaceful divorces: Czechoslovakia, the West Indies Federation, Serbia-Montenegro. It's true that the interspersing of populations can be a complicating factor. Yugoslavia is often cited as a textbook example of why partition is wrong, and the EU's determination to maintain the territorial integrity of Bosnia-Herzegovina is sometimes justified as an attempt to prevent a repeat of the horrors of the early 1990s. In fact, the way to have avoided those horrors would have been through a series of plebiscites, overseen by neutral observers. The resulting borders would have been almost exactly what they are now – with the difference that it might not have been necessary to fight a series of monstrous wars to secure them.

Had the international community accepted the case for national self-determination at the outset, and offered to mediate a series of votes and, where necessary, voluntary population exchanges, we might have been spared the horrors of war and ethnic cleansing. Instead, when Slovenia, in a referendum held on 23 December 1990, became the first state to declare independence, following a referendum in which 94.8 per cent of those taking part (and an extraordinary 88.5 per cent of all eligible voters) opted for secession, the EU responded by insisting on 'the territorial integrity of the Yugoslav federation'. It announced that any states which withdrew from the federation would be denied trade and aid accords. Only when the war had utterly destroyed the old state did it reluctantly recognise the reality of Croatian and Slovenian independence.[3]

The EU's distrust of the nation-state is perhaps most obvious in its relations with Israel. No country in the world so clearly embodies the national principle. For 2,000 years, Jews were scattered and stateless, but never lost their aspiration to statehood: 'Next year in Jerusalem'. If Israel's claim is valid – if people are truly better off living in their own national groups – then everything the EU has done since its foundation in 1956 is questionable. Which is why, in recent years, Brussels has shifted from a more-or-less uncomplicatedly pro-Palestinian position (the EU has long been the chief financial sponsor of the Palestinian entity in its various forms) to calling for regional integration and a dismantling of barriers – a process which, of course,

3 Noel Malcolm, *Bosnia: A Short History*, 1993.

poses a far more existential threat to the Jewish state. Israelis sometimes blame this attitude on anti-Americanism, or anti-Semitism. In fact, the EU is being perfectly consistent, rejecting national claims abroad as it does within its own territory.

In order to sustain the imperatives of integration, the EU is not only undemocratic in itself; it also requires its member nations to surrender a measure of their domestic accountability. As we shall now see, Charles de Gaulle was right in more ways than he knew.

3

– Why the EU Can't Be Democratic –

Democracy is not simply a periodic right to mark a cross on a ballot paper. It also depends upon a relationship between government and governed, on a sense of common affinity and allegiance. To put it another way, democracy requires a *demos*: a unit with which we identify when we use the word 'we'. Take away the *demos* and you are left only with the *kratos*: the power of a state that must compel by force of law what it cannot ask in the name of civic patriotism.

In the absence of a *demos*, governments are even likelier than usual to purchase votes through, for example, public works schemes and sinecures. Lacking any natural, patriotic loyalty, they have to buy the support of their electorates. One way to think of the EU is as a massive vehicle for the redistribution of wealth. Tax-payers in all the states contribute (though their contributions are hidden among the national tax-takes), and the revenue is then used to purchase the allegiance of articulate and powerful groups: consultants, contractors, big landowners, NGOs, corporations, charities, municipalities.

Unsurprisingly, the people running the EU have little time for the concept of representative government.

The (unelected) President of the European Commission, Jean-Claude Juncker, put it very pithily in the run-up to the Greek election in 2015: 'There can be no democratic choice against the European Treaties.'

Mr Juncker was restating the long-standing Brussels doctrine that European integration matters more than democracy. His predecessor, José Manuel Durão Barroso, used to contend that nation-states were dangerous *precisely because* they were democratic:

Governments are not always right. If governments were always right we would not have the situation that we have today. Decisions taken by the most democratic institutions in the world are very often wrong.
  – Speech in Berlin, 9 November 2011

This was, of course, a reaffirmation of de Gaulle's remark about democracy and national sovereignty being the same thing; the difference being that Mr Barroso saw both concepts as undesirable.

Which brings us to the gravamen of the case against the EU. It is contemptuous of public opinion, not by some oversight, but as an ineluctable consequence of its supra-national nature.

There is an old joke in Brussels to the effect that, if the EU were a country applying to join itself, it would be rejected on grounds of being insufficiently democratic. The joke understates the magnitude of the problem.

The EU is run, extraordinarily, by a body that combines legislative and executive power. The European Commission is not only the EU's 'government'; it is also, in most fields of policy, the only body that can propose legislation. Such a concentration of power is itself objectionable enough; but what is truly extraordinary is that the twenty-eight Commissioners are unelected.

Many supporters of the EU acknowledge this flaw. They call it the EU's 'democratic deficit', and vaguely admit that something ought to be done about it. But the democratic deficit isn't an accidental design-flaw; it is intrinsic to the whole project.

As we have seen, the EU's founding fathers had had a mixed experience with democracy – especially the populist and plebiscitary strain that came into vogue between the wars. Too much democracy was associated, in their minds, with demagoguery and fascism. There were, of course, differences of emphasis among them. The scheming Jean Monnet, who was never elected to public office, was more suspicious of the ballot box than his ascetic countryman Robert Schuman, who was twice prime minister of France. None the less, it is fair to say that the patriarchs prided themselves in creating a system where supreme power would be in the hands of 'experts': disinterested technocrats immune to the ballot box. They understood very well that a scheme as audacious as theirs, the merging of ancient kingdoms and republics into a single state, would never succeed if each successive transfer of power from the national capitals to Brussels had to be approved by the voters. They were therefore quite unapologetic about designing a system in which public opinion would be tempered or moderated by a bureau of wise men.

The EU's diffidence about representative government continues to this day, though it is not always articulated so blatantly as by Commissioner Juncker.

When, for example, referendums go the 'wrong' way, Eurocrats think nothing of swatting the results aside. When Denmark voted against the Maastricht Treaty in 1992, Ireland against the Nice Treaty in 2001, Ireland (again) against the Lisbon Treaty in 2008, people were told to go away and try again. When France and the Netherlands voted against the European Constitution in 2005, the verdict was simply disregarded.

When Greece voted against the bailout package in 2015, Mr Juncker first tried to warn Greeks that a 'No' vote would mean leaving the EU and then, when such a vote was delivered, simply disregarded it. Greece adopted the very bailout package, on precisely the same terms, that it had just rejected. As the German finance minister, Wolfgang Schäuble, put it: 'Elections change nothing.'

Not that anyone should have been surprised. After all, Mr Juncker had what the police call 'previous'. During the French and Dutch referendums in 2005, as Prime Minister of Luxembourg, he made clear that implementation would go ahead regardless of the outcome. When the results came in, he told MEPs: 'The French and Dutch did not really vote "No" to the European Constitution.'[1]

As in any abusive relationship, the contemptuous way in which Eurocrats treat voters has become self-reinforcing on both sides. The more voters are ignored, the more cynical and fatalistic they become. They abstain in record numbers, complaining – quite understandably – that it makes no difference how they cast their ballots. Eurocrats, for their part, are obliged to construct a world-view that justifies their readiness to defy the verdict of the urns. They fall quickly into the habit of treating public opinion as an obstacle to overcome rather than a reason to change direction. The imperatives of European integration require them to disregard popular majorities on the narrow issue of the EU; but this soon develops into a wider distrust of the masses.

To get around the awkward lack of enthusiasm for their project evinced by ordinary citizens, Euro-elites have developed a version of what Friedrich Engels called 'false consciousness'. Marxists used to contend that, if only the workers were in full possession of the facts, and free rationally to advance their own interests, they would vote for socialist parties. But in practice they were led astray by bourgeois interests. It was

1 *Daily Telegraph*, 17 July 2005.

therefore necessary for good Communists to act in the real, rather than the stated, interests of the majority.

How often one hears that argument, *mutatis mutandis*, in Brussels. If only people weren't hood-winked by Eurosceptic media barons; if only they weren't lied to by tabloids; if only they weren't whipped up by unscrupulous nationalists; if only there could be an informed and dispassionate election campaign. Then, *then* they would surely see that deeper integra-tion was in their interests. But because people are un-able to make an unclouded judgment, Eurocrats are entitled – obliged, indeed – to disregard the people's superficial desires in pursuit of their true preferences.

In his final interview as prime minister, Tony Blair offered a startlingly frank summary of the false con-sciousness doctrine:

The British people are sensible enough to know that, even if they have a certain prejudice about Europe, they don't expect their government necessarily to share it or act upon it.
– *Guardian*, 26 April 2007

Got that? We don't want our politicians to do as we say; we want them to second-guess our innermost, un-articulated desires. It need hardly be added that, from the point of view of the politician, this is a remarkably convenient theory.

Not all Eurocrats are cynics, of course. There are some idealists within the system: committed Euro-federalists who believe that it is possible to demo-cratise the EU without destroying it. Their ideal is a pan-European democracy, based on a more power-ful European Parliament. The scheme has been set out many times. The European Commission would become the Cabinet; the Council of Ministers would become the *Bundesrat* or Upper House, representing the nation-states; and the European Parliament would become the main legislative body. These were, indeed, the three specific proposals, put forward by Jacques Delors in 1990, that prompted Margaret Thatcher's famous response: 'No! No! No!'

Give MEPs more power, runs the theory, and people will take them more seriously. A higher cali-bre of candidate will stand, and turnout will rise. Pan-European political parties will contest the elections on common and binding manifestoes. People will add a European dimension to their political identity. It will, at this stage, no longer be necessary for Eurocrats to swat aside referendum results or impose policies with-out popular consent, because European democracy will have become a reality.

The problem with this idea is that it has already been tried, and has demonstrably failed. That failure can be inferred empirically from the turnout figures (see table overleaf).

Of those Europeans who had taken the trouble to register to vote before the June 2014 elections to the European Parliament, no fewer than 57.5 per cent

TURNOUT AT EUROPEAN ELECTIONS (PER CENT)

1979 – Nine members	62.0
1984 – Ten members	59.0
1989 – Twelve members	58.4
1994 – Twelve members	56.7
1999 – Fifteen members	49.5
2004 – Twenty-five members	45.6
2009 – Twenty-seven members	43.1
2014 – Twenty-eight members	42.5

declined to cast their ballots on the day. The figure is all the more remarkable when we consider that voting is compulsory in some member states, that others sought to boost participation by holding municipal elections on the same day, and that Brussels had spent hundreds of millions of euros on a campaign to encourage turnout.

Not that the abstention rate should have surprised anyone. There has, as we can see, been an unbroken decline in turnout since the first elections to the European Parliament were held in 1979. Still, the statistics are a serious embarrassment for Euro-integrationists. In the early days, they used to argue that the high abstention rate was a consequence of unfamiliarity, a function of the relative powerlessness of the new institution.

That theory has now been comprehensively disproved. Over the past thirty-five years, the European Parliament – like the EU in general – has been steadily agglomerating powers. Yet people have responded by refusing to sanction it with their votes. Back in 1979, when no one really knew what the European Parliament was, and Euro-elections were treated as a series of miniature referendums on national governments, turnout was disappointing rather than disastrous. The more familiar people have become with the EU, the further the turnout has fallen.

MEPs, naturally enough, respond to each new low by, in effect, blaming the electorate. They demand better information campaigns, more extensive (and expensive) propaganda. Europe, they declare, matters more than ever, and voters must be made to see it! It never occurs to them to infer any loss of legitimacy from the turnout figures, nor to devolve powers to a level of government that continues to enjoy democratic support. It is hard not to think of Bertolt Brecht's eerie lines: 'Wouldn't it therefore be easier to dissolve the people and elect another in their place?'

It won't do, either, to claim that turnout is falling in every democracy. It isn't. In the US, for example, it has risen from 49 per cent in 1996 to 55 per cent in 2012. Turnout at European elections is far lower than at national elections in the same countries, and is falling faster. Falling, we might add, for the most obvious of reasons: very few people think of themselves as Europeans in the same sense that they might think of themselves as Portuguese or Swedish. There is no pan-European public opinion, there are no pan-European media. You can't decree a successful democracy by bureaucratic fiat. You can't fabricate a sense of common nationality.

So far, so familiar. The undemocratic nature of the Brussels institutions has been a Eurosceptic complaint from the beginning. What is rarely appreciated is the extent to which, as well as being undemocratic within its own structures, the EU tends also to subvert the *internal* democracy of its member nations.

Consider a few examples. Ireland used to have exemplary laws on the conduct of referendums, providing for equal airtime for both sides, and the distribution of a leaflet with the 'Yes' and 'No' arguments to every household. When these rules produced a 'No' to the Nice treaty in 2001, they were revised so as to make it easier for the pro-EU forces to win a second referendum. That victory was duly secured, but a result was that *all* subsequent Irish referendums, not simply those to do with the EU, were fought on an unbalanced basis.

The same is true of Croatia, which dropped the minimum threshold provisions in its referendum rules in order to ensure entry into the EU in 2011.

When the President of the Czech Republic, Václav Klaus, declared that he was reluctant to sign the Lisbon Treaty into law, he was threatened with impeachment. He duly climbed down and, with poor grace, scrawled his name across the Bill; but, again, think of the precedent. From now on, any Czech President might face impeachment, not for impropriety, malfeasance or mental incapacity, but for sticking to the promises that he had very clearly made in the run-up to his election.

I could fill a book with similar cases: again and again, national democracy is vitiated in order to sustain the requirements of European integration. Borrowing a phrase from the title of one of C.S. Lewis's works of adult fiction, I think of the phenomenon as the EU's 'hideous strength'. The novel of that name tells of a diabolical plot that takes the guise of an apparently beneficent bureaucracy known as the National Institute for Co-ordinated Experiments (NICE). One by one, independent institutions find themselves subverted, bent to the will of the bureaucrats. In much the same way, national politicians repeatedly act against their personal, party and national interests for the sake of European integration.

When Ireland's referendum on the Lisbon Treaty was announced, the European establishment required the Taoiseach, Bertie Ahern, to stand aside lest the corruption allegations swirling around him destabilised the 'Yes' campaign. He was duly replaced with the most pro-EU member of his government, Brian Cowen. Cowen went on to lose anyway and then – in a move much applauded in Brussels – sided with the European Commission against his own electorate, demanding that people vote a second time. Once again, the EU got its way, in the sense that Ireland reversed its decision. But the price paid by Cowen's party was devastating.

Until the second Lisbon referendum, Fianna Fáil had been the fixed point in Ireland's party system, the star around which other parties orbited. It had won – in the sense of getting more votes than anyone else – every election since 1932, typically securing between 40 and 50 per cent of all ballots cast. In the 2011 general election, its share of the vote went from 41.6 to 17.4 per cent, as voters turned against a government that had meekly agreed to the EU's loans-for-austerity deal, saddling them with the cost of propping up the entire European banking system and turning Ireland into a vassal state.

The distortion of Ireland's democracy was just the beginning. Far more aggressive projections of the EU's hideous strength were to follow. November 2011 witnessed Brussels-backed coups in two EU member states – bloodless and genteel coups, but coups none the less. In Greece and in Italy, elected prime ministers were toppled and replaced with Eurocrats – respectively a former Vice-President of the European Central Bank, Lucas Papademos, and a former European Commissioner, Mario Monti.

The two premiers, George Papandreou in Greece and Silvio Berlusconi in Italy, had inadvertently stumbled into the path of the EU's combine harvester. Papandreou's mistake was to call for a referendum on Greece's austerity deal – a move which was to prompt purple, choking fury in Brussels where, as we have seen, the first rule is 'no referendums'.

Papandreou was not a Eurosceptic. On the contrary, he fervently wanted Greece to stay in the euro, and had planned to campaign for a 'Yes' vote. His sin, in the eyes of the Brussels establishment, was not to hold the wrong opinions, but to be too keen on democracy. Leninists had a term for party members who, though committed Bolsheviks, none the less behaved in a way that jeopardised the movement. They were called 'objectively counter-revolutionary'. Papandreou's reckless desire to consult the voters put him in this category; four days later, he was out.

Berlusconi, too, got on the wrong side of the EU's hideous strength. His pronouncement that 'since the introduction of the euro, most Italians have become poorer' was factually true, but sealed his fate. At a meeting in Frankfurt's opera house, Nicolas Sarkozy, Angela Merkel, Jean-Claude Juncker and the leaders of the IMF and ECB decided that the Italian premier was an obstacle to their plan to keep the euro together. We can hardly call it a secret plot: at the Cannes summit a few days later, officials were proudly wearing badges proclaiming their membership of the 'Frankfort Group'. One such official happily declared: 'We're on our way to moving out Berlusconi.'[2] If this was a conspiracy, it was what H. G. Wells called 'an open conspiracy'. Sure enough, a few days later, Berlusconi was gone, his exit triggered by a combination of a

2 *The Spectator*, 12 November 2011.

sudden withdrawal of ECB support for Italian bonds, verbal attacks from other EU leaders and a rebellion from Europhile Italian MPs.

It is true, of course, that both Papandreou and Berlusconi were already unpopular for domestic reasons – just as Margaret Thatcher had been when EU leaders and Conservative Euro-enthusiasts brought her down in November 1990. Had they been at the height of their powers, they would not have been vulnerable. None the less, to depose an incumbent head of government, even a wounded one, is no small thing.

Silvio Berlusconi, in particular, had survived a series of blows that would have felled anyone else. He had weathered accusations of bribery, soliciting underage sex, tax fraud and mafia links. He had shrugged off the attentions of – by his own count – 789 prosecutors and magistrates. He had laughed off gaffes on electric-rail topics from Muslims to Nazis. But he could not withstand the EU.

With Papandreou and Berlusconi out of the way, Brussels was able to install technocratic juntas in their place. Neither Lucas Papademos nor Mario Monti had ever stood for public office in his life. Mr Monti, indeed, managed to fill his Cabinet without appointing a single elected politician. Both men headed what were called 'national governments', but these administrations had been called into being solely to enforce programmes which their nations rejected. Both men derived their real mandates from their support in Brussels, and everyone knew it.

The most shocking aspect of the whole affair was that so few people were shocked. Two countries which, in living memory, had emerged from dictatorship were now suspending multi-party democracy. True, the outward forms of constitutionalism were observed: both new regimes were formally endorsed by parliamentary votes. Similar things could be said, though, by almost every tyrant in history, from Bonaparte onwards. The fact remained that these regimes existed for the narrow and explicit purpose of implementing policies that their peoples would throw out at a general election.

The Brussels system had been undemocratic from the start, but its hostility to the ballot box had always been disguised by the outward trappings of constitutional rule in its member nations. In 2011, that ceased to be true. Apparatchiks in Brussels now ruled directly through apparatchiks in Athens and Rome. The voters and their tribunes were cut out altogether. There was no longer any pretence.

4

– Falling for the Euro –

How did so many clever people get it so wrong? The flaws in the euro project are not just clear with hindsight; they were visible at the outset and were widely pointed out. It was never going to be possible to jam widely divergent economies into a single monetary policy. It was patently foolish to allow Italy and Greece to join with twice the permitted debt level. Yet, in every national parliament, in every central bank, in every university faculty, in every BBC editorial conference, there was a collective suspension of disbelief.

Why? What were supporters of the single currency thinking? If you listen carefully to what Euro-integrationists were saying at the time, you detect a subtext. It's not so much that they liked the euro, it's that they disliked the people who opposed it. Listen, for example to the then Lib Dem leader, Charles Kennedy, in 2002:

The euro, despite gloomy predictions from anti-Europeans, has proved to be a success. We cannot afford to be isolated from our biggest and closest trading partner any longer.

    – *Daily Telegraph*, 14 May 2002

Or to the chief of the Tory Europhiles, Ken Clarke:

Opponents of the euro have been disheartened as their predictions of chaos and disaster have failed to materialise. The
reality of euro has exposed the absurdity of many anti-
European scares while increasing the public thirst for information. Public opinion is already changing as people can see
the success of the new currency on the mainland.
— *The Times*, 15 May 2002

For such men, the issue was never really economic,
or even political, but tribal. Having defined the question, in their own minds at least, as a *Kulturkampf*
between sensible progressives and ignorant Blimps,
they became more or less uninterested in the facts. The
extraordinary thing is that many Euro-enthusiasts are
still at it, quite unabashed by how things have turned
out. Here, for example, is the historian Norman Davies
in the *Financial Times*, long after the consequences of
the euro had become clear:

'How marvellous,' they chortle in the Tory clubs; 'the busy-
bodies of Brussels are meeting their come-uppance. Greece
will push French banks down the chute first; but German
banks won't avoid it, and together they'll finish Italy off. With
luck, Italy will suck Spain into the abyss; Portugal will follow
Spain, and Ireland Portugal. Just think of it! Those Irish trai-
tors from 1922 will get their deserts! Terrific!'
Then continental banks lock their doors and the cash
machines dry up. Minestrone kitchens appear on the streets

of Rome. Spanish bullrings house the destitute. The bridges of Paris fill with rough sleepers. Weeks and months pass free of money. Europeans relearn the art of barter. When the cash flow stutters back, machines distribute drachmas again, the franc nouvel and the peseta nueva. Yet Britain's latterday Blimps will still not be satisfied. They hanker for the whole hog; before we pull up the drawbridge, they say, the EU itself must vanish.

    – *Financial Times,* 23 October 2011

For what it's worth, I have yet to meet a British Eurosceptic who is enjoying the economic turmoil on our doorstep. It is plainly in our interest that the eurozone – which takes forty per cent of our exports, and comprises our allies and friends – should flourish. That's precisely why we are alarmed at the readiness of Eurocrats to sacrifice their peoples' prosperity in order to keep the euro together.

Not that Norman Davies is much interested in what Eurosceptics actually think. One of the oddities of the whole debate is that commentators who are quick to spot prejudice in others when it comes to racism, sexism or xenophobia are quite unable to detect it in themselves when it comes to people who don't share their *Weltanschauung.*

None of this would matter if it were simply an academic debate. The trouble is that the people running the EU refuse to learn anything from the failure of their project. Since the crisis began, they have pursued only one policy: bailout-and-borrow. When it doesn't work, they accelerate it.

For years, EU leaders have been conditioned to spend public money. The first instinct of a Eurocrat, in a crisis, is to reach for his wallet – or, rather to reach for *your* wallet, since EU officials are exempt from paying national taxation. Expanding their budgets, of course, is what bureaucracies do best. As Mark Twain observed, if all you have is a hammer, everything starts to look like a nail.

Even so, there is something perverse about sticking to a policy which is manifestly failing in its stated objectives. Every new bailout is hailed as the end of the crisis. Every one fails, leaving the markets as sceptical as before, but increasing the mountain of outstanding debt.

Why this mulish determination to stick with a strategy that is impoverishing Europe? Some supporters of the project have fallen back on a cure-would-be-worse-than-the-disease shtick. They no longer try to argue that the euro has brought benefits – two thirds of the citizens who use it believe it has made them poorer, according to Eurobarometer – insisting instead that leaving would be impractical.

To British ears, such claims are eerily familiar. When it became clear that the Exchange Rate Mechanism, the euro's baleful predecessor, was wrecking our economy, the Establishment lined up to argue that, whatever the flaws in the system, we now had no option but to stick with it. Pulling out, declared John Major, would be 'the soft option, the inflationary option, the devaluer's option, a betrayal of the future of our country'.[1] In the event, of course, Britain's recovery began the day we left the ERM: 15 September 1992, four days after John Major's preposterous prediction. It's worth recalling this fact when John Major now makes near-identical claims about leaving the EU.

It's true that returning to national currencies would involve certain practical difficulties, but none would be insurmountable. By definition, all the countries in the euro have recently managed precisely such a changeover: that's how they joined in the first place. I don't remember any Eurocrats at that time droning on about the huge costs and complexities of having to replace your banknotes. And, indeed, the switch would be simpler now than it was a decade ago, because more money is digitised, and banknotes represent a smaller proportion of the currency in circulation.

I recently asked a Slovakian economist how his country had managed the monetary transition when it divorced the Czech Republic. 'Very easily,' he replied. 'One Friday, after the markets had closed, the head of our central bank phoned round all the banks and told them that, over the weekend, someone from his office would come round with a stamp to put on all their banknotes, and that, until the new notes and coins

1 *The Times*, 11 September 1992.

came into production, those stamped notes would be Slovakia's legal tender. On the Monday morning, we had a new currency.'

It's a little more complicated than that, but only a little. Why, then, do EU leaders persist in ruining Europe? Why are they inflicting deflation, poverty and emigration on the Mediterranean states, and open-ended tax rises on the northern states?

Because the euro was never about economics. It was and is about political union. The economic objections were never refuted; they were ignored as irrelevant. Which is why the people who made those objections – objections which, on every measure, have been vindicated – are not listened to. Who cares about unemployment? This was and is about the integration of Europe's formerly independent states.

I'm afraid there is no way to quote yourself modestly. Still, if only for the record, here is what I forecast in 1998, in a paper co-written with Mark Reckless:

The European Central Bank must set monetary policy according to the needs of the eurozone as a whole. An interest rate that is too high for the core members will be too low for the periphery. In reality, though, the core members are preponderant. In giving them the interest rate they need, the ECB can't help giving peripheral states a double-dose of what they don't need: low interest rates. The consequence will be an unsustainable credit boom in those states and, in due course, a commensurately painful crash.

– *The Euro: Bad for Business*, European Research Group

I mention this, not to say 'I told you so', but because of the spooky similarity between the arguments about joining the single currency in the late 1990s and those about remaining in the EU today.

We see precisely the same assertions being trotted out by precisely the same people. Going our own way, we are told, will mean loss of influence and economic decline and disinvestment.

Listen to what the leaders of the pro-EU movement said about joining the euro.

Sir Martin Sorrell, who put together the alliance of big corporations to lobby for EU membership in advance of the referendum, also organised a letter in 2003 which argued that failing to join the euro 'would be damaging for British-based businesses, British employees and the British economy as a whole'.

Sir Richard Branson, another prominent supporter of the pro-EU campaign, argued in 2000 that 'we cannot be members of the single market without also being members of the single currency, the euro' – an opinion which, rather eccentrically, he repeated as recently as 2015.

Tony Blair celebrated the launch of the euro in 1998 by saying that 'it marks the turning point for Europe, marks stability and growth and is crucial to high levels of growth and employment'. Well, he was right about the turning point – although in precisely the opposite way that he intended.

In 2003, Peter Mandelson said: 'Staying out of the

euro will mean progressive economic isolation for Britain. It will mean fewer businesses investing here, fewer good jobs being created and less trade being done with our European partners'. The last bit was true: British exports to the Eurozone have fallen as those countries have suffered, although our exports to the rest of the world have risen. But inward investment in the UK has been higher than anywhere else in the EU and, incredibly, Britain has created more new jobs since 2011 than the other twenty-seven members of the EU put together.

'As time goes on, people will increasingly see that there is a price to be paid for remaining outside the euro,' averred Neil Kinnock, now a big cheese in Labour's pro-EU campaign, back in 2002.

I could go on, but the point is clear enough. It's not just that the same people are making the argument. It's that the same people *are making the same argument*. Everything they now say about being outside the EU – that it would mean less inward investment, loss of influence, fewer jobs – is a repetition of what they said about being outside the euro. I can think of no political conflict where one side has been shown so comprehensively to be wrong, and yet has paid so low a price.

The euro was supposed to promote peace and amity among its participants. In reality, it has had the opposite effect. People are suffering in the downturn and are, quite understandably, blaming Brussels. Worse than that, they are blaming other countries, notably

Germany. Greek protesters regularly burn German flags and portray Mrs Merkel with Nazi insignia. The German press, perfectly reasonably, asks why German taxpayers should be expected to give money to Greece when this is the thanks they get. The single currency, in short, has brought relations between those two states to their worst pass since the end of the Second World War.

So if the euro is bad for prosperity *and* bad for friendship among nations, what is it for? Why do the Brussels elites cling so obsessively to the project? There surely must be more to it than inertia.

To answer that question, we need to understand the change in the nature of the EU bureaucracy: the way in which a once idealistic, or at least ideological, project has now become a way for a great many people to make a handy living.

5

– The Tyranny of the Status Quo –

W hen preparing the document that became the European Constitution, and then the Lisbon Treaty, the EU authorities made a great show of 'consulting the people'. In 2003, two hundred organisations, representing 'civil society' were invited to submit their suggestions on what the draft should contain. Interested in how these two hundred bodies had been selected, I put down a written question asking which of them received grants from the EU. After some toing and froing, the answer eventually came back: all of them.

You see how the system works? The EU sets up and funds an interest group. That group duly demands that the EU seize more powers. The EU then announces that, in response to popular demand, it is extending its jurisdiction.

Virtually every field of activity has some approved, EU-sponsored pressure group to campaign for deeper integration: the European Union of Journalists, the European Women's Lobby, the European Cyclists' Federation. These are not independent associations which just happen to be in receipt of EU funds. They are, in most cases, creatures of the European

Commission, wholly dependent on Brussels for their existence.

Nor is the racket limited to pan-European bodies headquartered in Brussels. The EU has been active in subsidising established NGOs within the nation-states, too. It starts harmlessly enough, with one-off grants for specific projects. After a while, the NGO realises that it is worth investing in a 'Europe officer' whose job, in effect, is to secure bigger grants. As the subventions become permanent, more 'Europe offic-ers' are hired. Soon, the handouts are taken for grant-ed and factored into the organisation's budget. Once this stage is reached, the EU is in a position to call in favours.

One example will serve to illustrate what I'm talk-ing about. When he introduced the Bill to ratify the Lisbon Treaty in 2007, the then Foreign Secretary, David Miliband made a great song and dance about the fact that it wasn't just Labour Europhiles who backed the text. A whole range of NGOs, he told the House of Commons, had also come out in favour:

'The NSPCC has pledged its support, as have One World Action, Action Aid and Oxfam,' he said, looking pleased with himself. 'Environmental organi-sations support the treaty provisions on sustainable development and even the commission of bishops sup-ports the treaty. This is a coalition, not of ideology, but integrity'.

Integrity? A few moments on the Internet revealed

that every organisation he had cited was in receipt of EU subventions. Most of them, it turned out, had also received grants from the British government. Hardly surprising, then, that they should dutifully endorse a treaty supported by their paymasters.

What *was* surprising was the extent of their financial dependency. When Mr Miliband sat down, I fired off a written question asking the European Commission how much money it had paid these organisations. It turned out that, in the previous year, ActionAid, the NSPCC, One World Action and Oxfam had between them been given €43,051,542.95.

Just think about that sum for a moment. Can organisations in receipt of such colossal subsidies legitimately call themselves 'non-governmental'? Can they claim to be independent? Can they even describe themselves as charities – at least in the sense that we commonly understand the word?

Why should any of us want to give money to a body that is already forcibly expropriating us through the tax system, and then using part of the revenue to lobby the government?

The other body which Mr Miliband cited, the 'commission of bishops', was a little harder to identify, but patient Googling revealed that its full name was the 'Commission of Bishops' Conferences of the European Community'. Far from being an episcopal body that just happened to back closer union, it was a Brussels-based outfit whose purpose was 'to promote reflection, based on the [Roman Catholic] Church's social teaching, on the challenges facing a united Europe'. In other words, while seeking to give the impression of broad support for a new transfer of powers to Brussels, the British Foreign Secretary was reduced to citing a body whose sole purpose is to interact with EU institutions, and which would be out of business if the EU disappeared. The French call the phenomenon *déformation professionelle*: the tendency, perhaps subliminally, to form opinions according to the dictates of your professional self-interest.

These various front organisations can even be dragged into arguments between different EU institutions. When, for example, the European Commission sought new Continent-wide rules on pesticides in 2007, it set up a front organisation called 'Pesticide Watch' – an amalgam of various EU-funded bodies – to push it in the direction it wanted. MEPs were then duly bombarded by emails from this campaign – presented, naturally, as missives from ordinary citizens.[1]

In much the same way, the Commission pays Friends of the Earth to urge it to take more powers in the field of climate change. It pays WWF to tell it to assume more control over environmental matters. It pays the European Trade Union Congress to demand more Brussels employment laws.

To summarise, the EU firehoses cash at its client

1 Speech to the European Parliament, Chris Heaton-Harris MEP, 27 October 2007.

organisations, these organisations tell it what it wants to hear, and it then turns around and claims to have listened to The People. And here's the clever bit: millions are thereby drawn into the system, their livelihoods becoming dependent on the European project.

We may be pretty certain that the organisations in receipt of Brussels cash will be in the forefront of the UK's 'Remain' campaign. And by no means only the charities and the NGOs. The CBI, which has become essentially a pro-EU pressure group, has received 936,272 euros. UK Universities, which campaigns strenuously for the EU, frankly admits that 'EU funding is too important to be sacrificed'. And you can almost see its point: since 2008, UK universities have had 889,889,754 euros from Brussels. But there is a fundamental flaw in the logic here. All that money was, in effect, deducted from Britain's contribution to the EU. If Britain withdrew, it could make the payment directly rather than routing it through Brussels. Or, if there really are advantages of scale in these international collaborations – as opposed to advantages to the officials who administer the grants – then the UK could remain involved with the EU funding programme in the way that non-EU Norway, Canada and Israel do.

While there are occasional grumbles against grants to this or that organisation, almost no one objects in principle to the shovelling around of public money in this fashion. Transparency campaigners sometimes complain about the influence of corporate lobbyists – and, of course, they are right. Oddly, though, they see a problem only on one side, refusing to acknowledge any parity between the green pressure groups and poverty campaigners on one side and the big business confederations on the other.

When the European Parliament voted in July 2011 on a Europe-wide reduction in carbon emissions, the then Environment Secretary, Chris Huhne, sanctimoniously ordered an investigation into the lobbying efforts of the energy companies. These companies had indeed been intruding aggressively into the debate: like all lobbyists, they had taken naturally to the EU system, grasping that it was designed by and for people like them. Far more energetic, though, had been the lobbying from their counterparts on the other side: Greenpeace, the WWF and Christian Aid.

The two sets of corporates are mirror images of each other. Both perceive that they can achieve far more in the Brussels institutions than they could *vis-à-vis* national parliaments, dependent as these legislatures are on public opinion.

Again, let me illustrate the attraction of the EU to special interests with a case study. Between 2007 and 2010, the EU proscribed several vitamin and mineral supplements and herbal remedies, and subjected others to a prohibitively expensive licensing regime. Opinions differ on the efficacy of alternative medicine, but no one tried to claim that the remedies in question were seriously deleterious to human health.

The reaction from consumers was immediate, negative and overwhelming. Some twenty million Europeans found that a harmless activity which they had pursued for years was being criminalised. I can't remember receiving so many letters and emails on any question in all my time in politics.

It is hard to imagine national legislatures, subject to the same electoral pressures, voting for such a ban. So Brussels became the target.

The target for whom? It was no secret. The restrictions were pushed strenuously by big pharmaceutical corporations. They could easily afford the compliance costs; their smaller rivals could not. Many independent herbalists, who had been in the habit of concocting creams and potions from their gardens, went out of business, and the big companies gained a near-monopoly.

Whenever Brussels proposes some apparently unnecessary and pettifogging rules, ask yourself *cui bono*? Who stands to benefit? Nine times out of ten, you will find that there is a company, or a conglomeration, whose products happen to meet all the proposed specifications anyway, and which sees the EU as a way to export its costs to its rivals.

Thus are businesses, as well as NGOs, drawn into the Euro-nexus. Thus are powerful and wealthy interest groups in every member state given a direct stake in the system.

The EU's strength is not to be found among the diminished ranks of true believers; not among the benign cranks who attend meetings of the European Movement or distribute leaflets for the Union of European Federalists. Nor, in truth, does it reside primarily among the officials directly on the Brussels payroll, either in the EU institutions or in its dozens of semi-detached executive bodies (the European Human Rights Agency, the European Space Agency, the European Police College and so on).

No, the real power of the EU is to be found in the wider corpus of interested parties: the businesses which are invested in the regulatory process; the consultants and contractors dependent on Brussels spending; the landowners receiving cheques from the CAP; the local councils with their EU departments; the seconded civil servants with remuneration terms beyond anything they could hope for in their home countries; the armies of lobbyists and professional associations; and, as we have seen, the charities and NGOs which, once they reach a certain size, almost always begin a financial relationship with the EU.

These are, of course, persuasive lobbies within their home countries. They tend to be made up of articulate professionals. No government lightly crosses them.

Nor are politicians immune to financial blandishments. It is common for former ministers to end up in EU jobs of one kind or another. Even heads of government often aim for such positions: several former prime ministers have wound up in the European Commission (José Manuel Barroso, Jean-Claude Juncker), in the European Parliament (Jean-Luc Dehaene, Silvio Berlusconi), or in the wider Eurocracy (John Bruton, the former Irish Taoseach, became the EU's Ambassador to Washington). Members of the European Parliament – trust me on this – receive a far more attractive financial package than legislators in any of the EU's national assemblies – even Italy.

The politicians, though, are vastly outnumbered by the corporate interests that have grown up around the EU. Theirs is the tiny public face of a swollen European *nomenklatura*.

One has to be careful when using such words as *nomenklatura*, of course. The EU is not the Soviet Union. It doesn't take away our passports or throw us into gulags; and, while it doesn't pretend to be democratic in its own structures, it rests ultimately upon the consent of twenty-eight democratic nations.

There is one sense, though, in which a parallel can be fairly drawn. The Communists who seized power in Central and Eastern Europe in the 1940s believed that the force of their ideology trumped any considerations of freedom, democracy or the rule of law. They saw Marxism-Leninism as both irrefutable and inexorable and, while they had no intention of allowing their doctrines to be rejected at the ballot box, many of them sincerely hoped that the suspension of democracy would be temporary. Once socialism had proved its superiority, once it had shown itself to be more economically efficient than capitalism as well as more just, it might be possible to move to a phased restoration of parliamentary rule.

Such reasoning was shaken by the Hungarian rising of 1956 and obliterated by the Prague Spring of 1968. After that date, the *apparatchiks* gave up trying to persuade their electorates. Instead of agreement, they demanded acquiescence; instead of conviction, consent. The dots and commas of *Das Kapital* became far less important than the maintenance of their place in society.

Something similar has happened to Eurocrats. In the early days, the Brussels institutions were dominated by true believers, convinced that, in burying nationalism, they were burying war. They, too, saw the lack of democracy as contingent: once the people saw the benefits of European integration, it would be possible to make the system more accountable. Their Prague Spring moment came in 2005, when 55 per cent of French voters and 62 per cent of Dutch voters rejected the European Constitution. The mood change in Brussels was immediate and palpable. One of my friends, a senior French Commission official, asked wretchedly: 'How can the voters have drifted so far away from me?' (It is human nature, I suppose, to place oneself at the centre of the universe.)

Since then, euro-*apparatchiks* have been defensive and tetchy. Like their Comecon counterparts in the 1980s, they have been more concerned with keeping

76

their positions than with winning the argument, less interested in altering public opinion than in avoiding it. Before the 'No' votes, they tried to convince themselves that Euroscepticism was essentially a British phenomenon, with perhaps a tiny offshoot in Scandinavia. Now, they know that almost any electorate will reject the transfer of powers to Brussels.

It was the great economist Milton Friedman who first used the phrase 'the tyranny of the status quo'. I wonder whether anyone who hasn't worked in government can fully appreciate the brilliance of his aperçu. The tyranny of the status quo is not simply a matter of people's innate conservatism, or of our psychological tendency to measure any proposition against the benchmark of current practice. It also rests upon the bureaucratic inertia that grows up around whatever happens to be the established dispensation.

Ask yourself this. If Britain were not already a member of the European Union – if our fathers had had the sense to negotiate a Swiss-style free trade agreement instead – would either of the two main parties now be arguing that we ought to join?

To put the question is to answer it. Why, then, is there such a consensus within the Establishment (as opposed to the country at large) in favour of continued membership? Precisely because it represents the status quo. For a great many important people, this is not a question of democracy or sovereignty, but a question of mortgages and school fees.

There is, as Adam Smith observed, 'a deal of ruin in a nation'. Or in a union. Just as the apparatchiks of Central and Eastern Europe clung to power for decades after the discrediting of their ideology and the collapse of whatever popular support they had enjoyed, so their European equivalents are in no hurry to stand aside for a cause so trivial as public opinion. How, then, is reform possible?

6

– Our Own Dream and
Our Own Task –

Every nation joins the EU for its own reasons. The French saw an opportunity to enlarge their *gloire*, *rang* and *prestige* (none of those words, interestingly, has precisely the same meaning in English). The Italians were sick of a corrupt and discredited political class. The good burghers of the Low Countries had had enough of being dragged *à contre cœur* into wars between their larger neighbours. The former Communist states saw membership as an escape from Soviet domination.

The German case is especially interesting. As we have seen, for German politicians of Chancellor Merkel's generation, the European project is beyond argument: a question of war and peace. It is important to understand the nature of this conviction.

German opinion-formers refer frequently, but always elliptically, to the Second World War. They talk of the EU as a way to 'avoid the worst in our history', or an alternative to 'the demons of the past'. In part, this indirectness is a way to avoid assertions which, if stated plainly, would sound ridiculous. A German politician who announced baldly 'If we don't give lots of money to the Greek government, we might find ourselves invading Poland', would, of course, be laughed at.

There is no question, though, that the sentiment is sincere and, in its own terms, wholly honourable. It is deeply offensive to characterise the EU as a German racket. One hears the charge all over Europe: from the French, from the Dutch, from Danes, Poles, Serbs, Czechs, Greeks, and, indeed, from Britons. In fact, Germany has never pressed her claims within the EU. She has been the largest net budgetary contributor from the beginning, yet is the most underrepresented state, in population terms, in the Brussels institutions. German taxpayers have uncomplainingly handed over a larger sum through the EU budget than ever their grandparents did under the Versailles reparation clauses, and have asked for no leadership role in return.

Their reticence is not simply a question of guilt or historical responsibility. Europe has also, in the eyes of many Germans, solved a national problem that had existed for hundreds of years.

A. J. P. Taylor, with the aggressive anti-Teutonic prejudice that animated many Leftists of his generation, defined the German question starkly. There were, he wrote, simply too many Germans. Such a numerous, disciplined and industrious people would, if fairly treated, inevitably dominate Europe. Their neighbours had therefore, over the years, found various ways to treat them unfairly – that is, to prevent them from fulfilling their national aspiration and living together in a single state. Since the Treaty of Westphalia, if not earlier, European coalitions had conspired to separate the German-speaking peoples – into fragmented princedoms, into separate Hohenzollern and Habsburg realms, into the FDR and DDR. This habit, A. J. P. Taylor concluded, naturally made Germans resent their treatment, and so made the region inherently unstable.

European integration seemed to offer the solution. Here, at last, was a way for Germany to be united and prosperous without threatening anyone. As long as neighbouring states felt that Germany was, in some sense, their country too, as long as they felt a stake in her success, they would not resent her numerical or industrial preponderance.

In 1990, Helmut Kohl declared 'European unity and German unity are two sides of the same coin'. That sentence makes little sense except in the context just described. What the Chancellor was telling his countrymen was that, by creating a united European polity, he and his fellow leaders would also create a dispensation in which a united Germany would be accepted by her former enemies.

It would be churlish not to acknowledge the appeal of this argument, especially to those who grew up immediately after the Second World War. Germany in 1945 was ravaged and dishonoured. Her infrastructure had been bombed to wreckage, her reserves were exhausted, her people were hungry, she had again been partitioned, and there were foreign armies garrisoned on her soil. Had an aspirant politician clambered onto some clump of bricks by the ruined Reichstag and prophesied that, within fifteen years, Germans would be the most prosperous people in Europe, that they would be valued Nato allies, that they would have the economic leadership of the Continent and that none of their neighbours would resent or fear their recovery, he would have sounded like a madman. For Germans over a certain age, Europe was the totem that effected this magical transformation. No wonder it is beyond criticism.

Germany is, perhaps, an extreme case. But one thing that is common to almost all EU members is that they joined out of a sense of pessimism. Confident and prosperous nations, such as Norway and Switzerland, see no need to abandon their present liberties. Less happy nations seek accession out of, if not despair, pre-cisely, then a sense of national angst. Sweden joined immediately after a banking collapse. Iceland regis-tered a pro-EU majority only for five bleak months fol-lowing the meltdown of her financial sector; the polls swung back as the immediate crisis passed.

Britain joined at what was, on most measures, her lowest moment as a modern nation. Between 1945 and 1973 – the year she became a member – Britain had been comprehensively outperformed by every Western European economy outside Iberia. In retrospect, we can see that a great deal of this decline had to do with the war debt: Britain had amassed colossal liabilities during the struggle against Hitler and, for the next three decades, this debt was a drag on growth. Successive governments chose to inflate their way out of trouble which, of course, had a knock-on effect on productivity. By the 1970s, decline seemed irremediable. Britain suffered from double-digit inflation, constant strikes, the three-day week, power cuts and prices and incomes policies. It was during this black period that Parliament passed the European Communities Act in 1972, a decision confirmed in Britain's first national referendum in June 1975, which resulted in a two-to-one 'Yes' vote. It is hard to imagine a similar outcome had that referendum been held either ten years earlier or ten years later; the necessary sense of national pessimism would have been lacking.

It is worth noting, as an aside, that Britain's timing could hardly have been worse. Western Europe had indeed grown spectacularly between 1945 and 1973. Part of this growth was a bounce back from the artificial low of the Second World War. Infrastructure had been destroyed, but an educated and industrious workforce remained in place. There was also a mass movement of people, from the countryside to cities, from the Mediterranean to the coalfields of northern countries, and from former colonies to Europe. Europe, moreover, profited from massive external assistance. Thirteen billion dollars were disbursed under Marshall Aid, coming on top of the twelve billion dollars separately contributed by the US between 1948 and 1952. Arguably even more valuable was the US defence guarantee, which allowed European governments to divert military spending to civil projects.

Sadly, from Britain's point of view, this relative growth came to a halt shortly after she joined. Western Europe lost its lead during the 1974 oil crisis, and never really recovered. In 1973, the year of Britain's accession, Western Europe – defined for these purposes as the fifteen members of the EU prior to the admission of the former Communist countries in 2004 – accounted for 38 per cent of world GDP. In 2010, that figure was 24 per cent. In 2020, it will be 15 per cent.[1]

Far from joining a growing and prosperous free trade area, the United Kingdom confined herself in a cramped and declining customs union. And, in doing so, she stood aside from her natural hinterland: the markets of the Commonwealth and the wider Anglosphere, which have continued to grow impressively as Europe has dwindled. It is hard not to think of the lament of the Prussian general when he first saw Austro-Hungarian troops in action in 1914: 'We have shackled ourselves to a corpse'.

Every country had her own motive for being involved with the European endeavour, but Britain was none the less in a separate category. Her initial assumptions about democracy, sovereignty and the role of the

1 US Department of Agriculture, 2010.

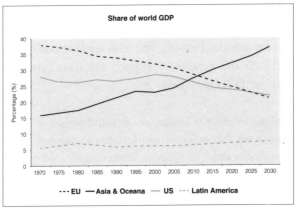

Share of world GDP

Source: Economic Research Service of the U.S. Department
of Agriculture, *International Macroeconomic Data Set*

nation-state differed fundamentally from those of the other members. She was the only European country to have fought in the Second World War without, at one time or another, losing. In consequence, she did not begin in 1945 with a sense that her political institutions had failed. She did not, as many European states did, rewrite her constitution, so as to start afresh. And, of course, she did not share in the belief that patriotism was a dangerous and undesirable force. Across much of the Continent, self-proclaimed patriots had been tainted by their association with fascism. In Britain, by contrast, national loyalties had been the focus of resistance against the Nazi tyranny.

Britain was different in another important way. While she was connected by geography to Europe, she was pulled by habit and history, by language and law, by kinship and commerce, towards more distant continents. This was, indeed, General de Gaulle's reason for vetoing Britain's first two applications to the EEC. As the general explained, when justifying his '*non*' on 14 January 1963:

England in effect is insular, she is maritime, she is linked through her exchanges, her markets, her supply lines to the most diverse and often the most distant countries; she pursues essentially industrial and commercial activities, and only slight agricultural ones. She has in all her doings very marked and very original habits and traditions.

His veto was regarded by British opinion-makers at the time as an act of stunning ingratitude toward the country that had sheltered him during the Nazi occupation. But perhaps the general had a finer appreciation for the instincts of the British people than had their contemporary leaders. His reasoning has stood the test of time remarkably well:

Can Great Britain now place herself like the Continent and with it inside a tariff which is genuinely common, renounce all Commonwealth preferences, cease any pretence that her agriculture is privileged, and, more than that, treat her engagements with other countries of the free trade area as null and void? That is the whole question.

That question has never found a wholly satisfactory answer. Twenty-five years later, Margaret Thatcher made essentially the same argument as the General, albeit less diplomatically, when she observed that, throughout her life, Britain's problems had come from Europe, and the solutions from the rest of the English-speaking world.

She spoke for her generation. More than a hundred million men from the Empire and Commonwealth had volunteered to serve in the two wars. Alliance in adversity had created a sentimental bond which was strengthened by family connections. At first, these links came from emigration. Later, they were to come from immigration, too. Britain might be just 22 miles from the Continent, but her airmail letters and, later, her international telephone calls, went overwhelmingly to North America, the Caribbean, the Indian sub-continent, Australia and New Zealand.

It was not surprising that Britain had little enthusiasm for a project that involved the creation of an internal European market at the expense of global commercial links. Britain conducted a far higher proportion of her trade with non-European states than did any other member.

It would no doubt have surprised most policy-makers in 1973 to see that the UK's sales to the EU are now dropping precipitately. Immediately after 1973, as the Common External Tariff was imposed in stages, Britain's trade was artificially redirected from global markets to Western Europe.

In time, though, this redirection was more than

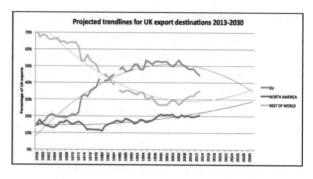

offset by the EU's relative decline – a decline that has, of course, been speeded by the euro crisis. Supporters of EU membership like to claim that 'around half our trade' is with the EU. But that 'around' is tendentious. In 2007, the EU took 54 per cent of Britain's exports in goods and services; in 2015, that figure had fallen to 44 per cent. What will it be in 2030? Or 2040? Will we still be having a debate about whether to merge our political institutions into the EU when it takes, say, a quarter of our exports?

At this point, Euro-enthusiasts generally shift their ground. It isn't only about sales, they say; it's also about influence. Had Britain been more enthusiastic when the EEC was established, perhaps the rules might have been set in a way more conducive to our interests. Let us not repeat that mistake, they argue, by walking away now.

The myth of a stand-offish Britain has taken root so deeply that it is almost past the point of correction. Still, it is worth reiterating the facts. Britain was deeply involved with, and committed to, the recovery of Western Europe after 1945. The Attlee Government voluntarily passed 25 per cent of its Marshall Aid money to Germany, which was close to starvation. Britain was an enthusiastic – arguably the most enthusiastic – supporter of Nato and the Council of Europe, both founded in 1949.

It was not European collaboration that Britain objected to; quite the contrary. Her objection, rather, was to the particular model of integration favoured by the Euro-federalists.

Throughout the early 1950s, Britain argued for the creation of a broad European free trade area, based on the seventeen-member Organisation for European Economic Cooperation – now the OECD. Such a body should, British diplomats proposed, remain closely linked to the United States and open to trade with the rest of the world. In particular, it should not artificially drive up the cost of food by creating a protected European farming sector, with prices regulated by the state.

These proposals, in the event, served to spur the federalist countries into pushing ahead more quickly. Fearing the prospect of dilution, they determined on a small, tight community, based on a common external tariff, industrial and agrarian support and common political institutions. It is often said that these things happened only as a consequence of Britain having absented herself from the negotiations. Had the UK joined at the start, the Europhile narrative goes, Europe might have developed in a far more flexible and free-trading direction.

But Britain *was* involved in the discussions: her plan for a broad European free trade area, while it found no support in the old Carolingian states, was backed by the Scandinavian countries as well as by her old ally Portugal. In 1955 at the Messina Conference, Britain made one last attempt to divert Europe onto a more liberal path, arguing for a common market based on mutual product recognition, rather than a customs union based on uniform standards. (The British proposal was known, in the diplomatic jargon of the time, as 'Plan G'.) The federalist countries responded by agreeing a scheme that might have been specifically designed to keep the British out. Their tariff walls were especially prejudicial to Britain, which was in the habit of importing its food and raw commodities from the Commonwealth. The political institutions were especially alien to Britain's Westminster traditions. When the Common Agricultural Policy was agreed in 1960, it was based around supporting the smallholdings common in France and Bavaria. For Britain, a net food importer with relatively large and efficient farms, it would plainly be disastrous.[2]

No British government could join on such terms. Yet the Treaty of Rome did not end the

2 Martin Schaad, *Contemporary European History*, 1998.

discussions. Britain continued to negotiate with the Six, applying for membership five years later under Harold Macmillan, and again seven years after that under Harold Wilson. Both times, the negotiations broke down over the issues that had precluded Britain's involvement in the first place: access for Commonwealth exports, political union and the Common Agricultural Policy.

It was at this stage that Edward Heath, perhaps the most uncritical Euro-integrationist ever to have sat in Parliament, became leader of the Conservative Party and in 1970, much to the country's surprise, prime minister. Heath, who had been the chief negotiator during Macmillan's unsuccessful membership bid, was determined to get in on any terms. His fanaticism marked him out even from the other Europhiles on the Tory front bench: Iain Macleod, Reginald Maudling, R. A. Butler.

It is hard to imagine any other politician being prepared to sacrifice so much in order to join. Heath acquiesced in full to the EU's agricultural and in-dustrial policies, its external protectionism and its anti-Americanism. He not only accepted, but loudly applauded, its ambition to become a single federal state. So abject was his attitude that, in the hours be-fore joining, he handed away Britain's fishing grounds as a sort of late entry fee. Under maritime law, 70 per cent of the fish stocks in the North Sea were in British territorial waters. Under the Common Fisheries Policy,

Britain was allocated a quota equivalent to 25 per cent by volume or 15 per cent by value. Indeed, Heath was even content to accept that the EU should carry on using its existing four official languages, French, German, Italian and Dutch. It was only at the insistence of Irish negotiators that English, too, was included.

It seems clear that Britain could have joined on such terms at any time. The metaphors about missing trains and boats and buses all miss the point. To argue that the EU might have developed in a less federalist and less *dirigiste* way had the United Kingdom been present from the start is to beg the question. It was precisely because the authors of the project were determined on these goals that Britain was excluded.

In the circumstances, it was inevitable that the British people would have a different approach to European integration. The British authorities never tried to sell the project to their electorate as being primarily about peace. Instead, they appealed to the free-trading instincts of a merchant nation. The EEC was rechristened the 'Common Market'. Membership was advanced as a wholly economic proposition. Even Edward Heath, the most committed Euro-federalist of his era, had the sense to downplay the political aspirations of the other states. His nickname, The Grocer, came from his tendency to read out price lists, seeking to demonstrate that essential household goods were cheaper on the Continent than in Britain. The implications for sovereignty were not simply minimised;

they were expressly denied. In a television broadcast
to mark Britain's formal accession to the EEC in 1973,
the Prime Minister declared:

There are some in this country who fear that in going into
Europe we shall in some way sacrifice independence and sovereignty. These fears, I need hardly say, are completely un-
justified.
 – BBC broadcast, 2 January 1973

That statement has been thrown back at the Conservative Party ever since. People felt, with reason, that
they had been deceived by their leaders, that they had
joined on a false premise. Instead of becoming members of what they had assumed to be a common market, based on the free circulation of goods and mutual
recognition of products, they had joined a quasi-state
which was in the process of acquiring all the trappings
of nationhood: a parliament, a currency, a legal system,
a president, a diplomatic service, a passport, a driving licence, a national anthem, a foreign minister, a
national day, a flag.

At the same time, the common market itself never
properly materialised. As we have seen, the European
Commission was keener on standardisation than on
mutual product recognition. Rather than ruling that
if, say, a bottle of mineral water was legal in Britain,
it might also be legally sold in Italy and vice versa,
the EU tended to lay down precise specifications: that

the bottle should have a volume of not less than X and not more than Y, that certain minerals had to be included and certain others excluded and so on. Manufacturers and retailers who had no export trade – and the majority of firms do business within a ten-mile radius of where they are sited – might none the less find their product prohibited. Instead of expanding consumer choice, the European authorities were restricting it.

We can say with some certainty that the costs of regulation in the EU outweigh the benefits of the single market. The reason we can be sure is that we have the figures from the European Commission itself. The Commission tells us that the single market boosts the EU's GDP by 120 billion euros a year. We might cavil at this figure, of course: the Commission is hardly a disinterested assessor; it has every reason to talk up the numbers. None the less, let us be generous and allow, for the sake of argument, that that figure is accurate. In November 2004, the then Internal Market Commissioner, Guenther Verheugen, asked his department to assess the total cost of business regulation in the EU. The answer? Six hundred billion euros a year. Thus, by the Commission's own admission, the economic costs of the EU outweigh the benefits fivefold.[3]

Britain was not the only state to have joined for largely economic reasons. Ireland and Denmark joined

3 *EU Competitiveness Report*, 5 November 2004.

on the same day, largely as a consequence of British accession. Sweden, too, saw membership as being essentially about market access. In all of these countries, the mood turned as the promised benefits failed to materialise.

It was Britain, though, where the reaction was strongest. This was partly because the cost-benefit analysis was more clearly negative for the UK than for any other state. Britain has paid more into the EU budget than she has received back in forty-one out of forty-two years of membership (the exception being 1975: the year of the referendum on withdrawal). Indeed, for most of those forty-two years, there were only two net contributors: Britain and Germany.

Britain was doubly penalised by the Common Agricultural Policy: as a net food importer with an efficient farming sector, she was hit both positively and negatively, paying more in and getting less back.

She was, of course, uniquely deleteriously impacted by the Common Fisheries Policy which, for the

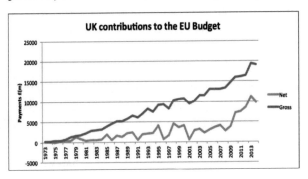

next thirty years, did not apply to the Mediterranean or the Baltic, but only to the North Sea. It was, in other words, an overtly anti-British policy.

And, of course, her trade suffered/1973 saw Britain wrenched from her natural trading partners. Until that year, she had imported food and raw materials from the Commonwealth, and exported finished products. In the years that followed, Commonwealth free trade was replaced with the Common External Tariff. Commerce was artificially redirected to the European continent. Glasgow, Bristol and, in particular, Liverpool were suddenly on the wrong side of the country, and their docks went into decline.

Britain had until then run a trade surplus with the existing EEC members, the Six. In 1973, that trade went into deficit, where it has remained to this day. Indeed, over the forty-two years of her membership of the EU, Britain has run a cumulative trade surplus with every continent in the world except Europe. She has had to make up, through her exports to North America, South America, Africa, Asia and Australia, the current account deficit she runs with the EU.

In September 2011, at a *Spectator* debate in London, I argued the merits of EU membership with the former Europe Minister, Denis MacShane. Denis came up with one of the more common, yet more puzzling, arguments for staying in. 'What you have to understand, Danny [he always calls me Danny for some reason], is that we sell more to Belgium than we do to the whole of India.' That, I replied, was precisely our problem. Which of those two markets represents the better long-term prospect?

This is not an argument peculiar to Britain. There has always been something curiously artificial about creating a single market in Europe at the expense of broader global commercial relationships. The whole point of a market, after all, is to swap on the back of differences. The more heterodox the market, the greater the benefits. Why, then, form a market exclusively out of similar industrialised European economies? And why, even more perversely, pressure other regions of the world into doing the same thing? Why, to pluck an example more or less at random, does the EU insist that the nations of Central America participate in their own regional trade bloc, complete with its supranational parliament ('Parlacen')? Why does it refuse to sign trade or aid deals with individual states in the region unless they join this bloc? What possible advantage is there to the Central Americans in selling each other the products which they all produce: bananas, coffee, cut flowers?

The answer, of course, is that none of these initiatives is really about trade. All are about spreading the ideology of political integration as a desirable aim in itself.

What makes Britain unusual in the EU is not that it suffers especially badly from these policies. For a long time, it did, but the euro crisis has made it impossible to sell the EU as an economic proposition in any of the twenty-eight states. No, what sets Britain apart is that the EU has only ever been presented here as an economic proposition. Unlike in, say, Germany, there is no reservoir of European sentiment to tap.

The United Kingdom has spent forty years conducting the fundamental argument about Europe which other states are only now beginning. Britain's institutions, temperament, size and experience equip it, as perhaps no other EU member, to seek a fundamentally different relationship with Brussels. Once it sets the precedent, however, others will surely follow, and Europe might yet be rescued from her current discontents.

'England will save herself by her exertions,' declared William Pitt in 1805, 'and will, as I trust, save Europe by her example.'

7

– And We Have Not Spoken Yet –

W hat is the alternative to EU membership? We could do worse than to begin with some of the existing options. Several countries are part of the single market without being full members of the EU, ranging from the Channel Islands and Liechtenstein to Iceland and Turkey. While each has its own particular deal with Brussels, all have managed to negotiate unrestricted free trade while standing aside from the political institutions.

Consider, as an example, Switzerland. The Swiss rejected membership of the European Economic Area – intended as a precursor to full EU membership – in a referendum in December 1992. Although almost all the political parties had campaigned for a 'Yes' vote, they accepted the verdict, and set out to negotiate an alternative arrangement with the EU. Over the next three years, they negotiated a series of sectoral accords covering everything from fish farming to the permitted size of lorries on highways. More recently, they also signed up to the EU's passport-free area, the Schengen Accord, which the UK and Ireland have declined to join.

The result of these negotiations is that the Swiss

have all the advantages of commercial access without the costs of full membership. The issue has, in consequence, disappeared from the political agenda there.

Switzerland participates fully in the four freedoms of the single market—free movement, that is, of goods, services, people and capital. But she is outside the Common Agricultural and Fisheries Policies and pays only a token contribution to the EU budget.

It is true, of course, that Swiss exporters must meet EU standards when selling to the EU – just as they must meet Japanese standards when selling to Japan. But they are not obliged to apply every pettifogging Brussels directive to their domestic economy.

Critically, Switzerland is also free to sign trade accords with third countries, and often does so when she feels that the EU is being excessively protectionist. Switzerland negotiated a bilateral Free Trade Agreement with China in 2014, for example, and is currently negotiating one with India.

Britain, by contrast, is bound by the Common External Tariff, and is often prevented from adopting a more liberal position by the interest of a cosseted producer elsewhere in the EU. When the EU engages in bra wars with China or shoe wars with Vietnam, it is usually for the sake of protecting industries in Southern Europe. The United Kingdom is perforce drawn into these disputes; Switzerland is not.

Here, though, is the clinching statistic. In 2014 the Swiss exported five times as much per head to the

EU as the British did. So much for the notion that our exports to the continent depend on our participation in the EU's institutional structures.

Might the other member states discriminate against our exports if we left? Hardly. We would still be covered by World Trade Organisation and, indeed, European Economic Area rules. More to the point, Britain's trade with the EU, which was in surplus before we joined, has been in deficit during forty-one of the forty-two subsequent years. In 2014, the UK ran a colossal £61.6 billion trade deficit with the EU – as compared to a £27.8 billion surplus with the rest of the world.[1]

Our trade deficit is not in itself, of course, a reason to leave the EU. But it gives the lie to any notion that the other members would seek to restrict the cross-Channel commerce from which they are the chief beneficiaries. In any commercial transaction, the customer tends to have a stronger position than the salesman.

Britain should maintain her trade links with the Continent, her intergovernmental co-operation and her military alliance. We cannot but be interested in the affairs of our neighbours. At the same time, though, we should raise our eyes to more distant horizons and rediscover the global vocation that our fathers took for granted.

I have noticed, when debating this question over

1 *City AM*, 26 June 2015 – the figures for 2015 are not available at the time of writing.

many years that we often engage in a dialogue of the deaf. Supporters of the EU invariably conflate political participation with access to the European market. Many, indeed, seem genuinely to have convinced themselves that the two things are identical.

It is worth stressing that no one – *no one* – is suggesting that Britain should disengage from European trade. Withdrawal from the EU does not imply withdrawal from the European market. Indeed, under Article 50 of the Lisbon treaty, the EU is obligated to negotiate a commercial accord with any state that leaves.

In 2014, the EU ratified its Association Agreements with Moldova and Ukraine, meaning that there is now a truly pan-continental free trade area. From non-EU Iceland to non-EU Turkey, goods and services circulate without tariffs or trade barriers. There are almost as many non-EU participants in this market as there are EU members. Indeed, the only two geographically European states which have chosen to stand aside are Belarus and Russia. No one in Brussels – and no one in Britain other than in the press releases of pro-EU campaigners – has ever suggested that Britain would leave such a market simply because it withdrew from the EU's political institutions.

Britain might choose to remain in the European Economic Area, like Norway. Norwegian exports to the EU in 2010 were twice as much per head as Britain's. Or it might prefer to leave the EEA, too, and rely on bilateral free-trade accords, like Switzerland. To repeat – for this fact cannot be repeated too often – Swiss exports to the EU in 2010 were *five times as much per head as Britain's*.

Some protest that, while this might be the legal position, an acrimonious split could leave the EU looking for ways to erect unofficial non-tariff barriers against British trade. Why on earth should it want to do so, though, when the balance of such trade is overwhelmingly to the advantage of Continental exporters? Over the past forty years, Britain has run a cumulative trade surplus with every continent on the planet except Europe. Between 2005 and 2010, the EU accounted for 92 per cent of our total trade deficit.[2] It is hard to imagine that other EU states would wish to prejudice their trade with what would be, by a long way, their single biggest export market.

As for the idea that we are too small to survive on our own, it rests on a misconception. We saw in Chapter One that the most prosperous people in the world tend to live in tiny countries. In global wealth league tables, the ten states with the highest GDP per capita all have populations below seven million. What matters to a modern economy is not its size, but its tax rate, its regulatory regime and its business climate. One of the reasons the EU's GDP is shrinking as a proportion of world GDP is that deeper integration means less

2 *Global Britain, The EU and the Deficit*, 2011.

competition among the member states, which in turn means higher taxes and more regulation.

Too small to survive? Britain is the fifth largest economy in the world, the fourth largest military power and the fourth largest exporter. It is a member of the G8 and one of five members of the UN Security Council. It enjoys close links to America and the Commonwealth (which, unlike the EU, is growing impressively). If seven million Swiss and four million Norwegians are able, not simply to survive outside the EU, but to enjoy arguably the highest living standards on Earth, surely sixty-five million Britons could manage.

The odd thing is that, as the argument has moved on to economic territory, supporters of the EU have shifted their ground. It is not really about trade after all, they say. Rather, it is about having influence in the world.

Alright then. At the risk of stating the obvious, you have a more influential foreign policy when you have a foreign policy in the first place. Again, consider the EFTA states, Switzerland and Norway. The fact that Switzerland is not in the EU does not seem to have deterred the World Health Organisation, the International Olympics Committee, the International Labour Organisation, FIFA or hundreds of other global bodies from basing themselves on Swiss soil.

Norwegian diplomats are arguably the most proportionately influential in the world, having played a role in peace talks in Sudan, South-East Asia, Sri

Lanka and Israel-Palestine. I remember talking to the Norwegian ambassador to London in 1994, just after his country had voted against EU membership. 'Before the referendum,' he told me, 'we were treated as a kind of extra EU state. I'd be invited everywhere with the other fourteen ambassadors, and often I wouldn't even get the chance to speak. Since the "No" vote, people have had to deal with me again.'

Britain has eight times the population of Switzerland and twelve times that of Norway. The idea that we maximise our influence by contracting it out to the EU institutions simply does not stand up.

What has perhaps changed most radically of all is technology. In the 1950s, regional blocs were all the rage. So, for that matter, were conglomerates of every sort: in business, in politics, in the trade union movement. Wise-sounding men asserted authoritatively that the world was dividing into blocs, and that it would be a foolish country that found itself left out.

Even as late as the 1970s, when Britain joined, this argument seemed plausible. Europe had embarked on economic integration and had, until that moment been doing rather well. People understandably, if incorrectly, attributed its growth to its amalgamation rather than to the factors discussed in the last chapter: large-scale migration, US assistance and, above all, the bounce back from an artificial low in 1945.

Nowadays, though, distance has ceased to matter. Capital surges around the globe at the touch of a button.

The Internet has brought the planet into a continuing real-time conversation. Geographical proximity has never mattered less.

A company in my constituency will as easily do business with a firm in Dunedin, on the opposite side of the planet, as with one in Dunkirk, twenty-five miles away. The New Zealand company, unlike the French one, will be English-speaking, will have similar accountancy practices and unwritten codes of business ethics. Should there be a misunderstanding or dispute, it will be arbitrated in a manner familiar to both parties. None of these things is true across the EU, despite half a century of harmonisation. Technological change is making the EU look like the 1950s hangover it is.

What would happen if the United Kingdom negotiated an amicable divorce? Britain itself, we can be reasonably certain, would be better off. But what would be the impact on the Continent? How many other nations might demand a similarly reformed relationship? By constantly focusing on the effects of EU withdrawal on Britain, we neglect the effects of British withdrawal on the EU. Britain would become, overnight, the EU's largest trading partner and most important neighbour. The European dynamic would be wholly altered.

Ireland and Denmark joined on the same day as the United Kingdom, and did so largely because of Britain's application. Thirteen years later, Portugal, too, joined her oldest ally. Sweden acceded twelve years after that and, while there were several factors at stake in her decision, it is hard to imagine that the issue would have been considered had the UK and Denmark not already been members. Something similar might be said another twelve years on of Estonia, Latvia and arguably Malta.

That's not to say that these countries would promptly reconsider their membership the moment Britain left. Whatever the original rationale of their applications, they are as subject to Friedman's 'tyranny of the status quo' as anyone else. In Copenhagen and in Tallinn, just as in London, a caste of well-remunerated Eurocrats is prepared to fight for its privileges.

None the less, the removal of the United Kingdom would tilt the balance fundamentally in favour of the federalist states, above all the core, Carolingian countries and their satellites. Many of the more free-trading nations on the periphery would become uneasy. I don't think it is unreasonable to look forward to a separating-out: a division between a federalist core and a more commercial periphery.

As we saw in Chapter Four, this separation might well be beginning anyway as a result of the euro crisis. The notion that all EU member states must accept a common outcome – *le finalité politique* in the jargon – has been overtaken by events. Membership of the euro, and of its associated rules on fiscal union, creates a political dynamic of its own. Various schemes for political combination, instead of being pursued in a desultory way by all members, will be embraced enthusiastically by some. The countries outside the euro will increasingly find that they are excluded from much else – to the horror of their professional diplomats, but the approval of their populations. There will come a moment when formally withdrawing from the EU's political structures – the European Commission and Parliament – and instead setting up EFTA-style joint authorities will seem a natural step.

Which countries are we talking about? The answer will of course depend on who is in power at the time in the various national capitals. We can though, point to certain states which, by their inclination and temper, tend to look out beyond the European continent.

At the start of his beautiful book *Voltaire's Coconuts*,[3] the Anglo-Dutch writer Ian Buruma recalls finding an old guidebook in the Netherlands which had been published by the Wehrmacht during the German occupation. Among other things, it argued that, while the Eastern Dutch were proper Aryans who might eventually be assimilated into the Reich, the coastal Dutch were hopelessly mercantile, Anglophile and debased.

Buruma agreed, albeit, obviously, from the opposite perspective. Indeed, he extended the argument to Europe as a whole, identifying Anglophile (and, by extension, Atlanticist) Europe as the free-trading littoral:

3 *Voltaire's Coconuts or Anglomania in Europe*, Ian Buruma, 2000.

the Hanseatic cities, Norway and Denmark, the Netherlands, Flanders, Portugal.

These places have tended, over the years, to be sturdy and self-governing; to resent the power of distant kings; to value their civic privileges; to develop mechanisms of representative government; to favour open markets over state power. They have, in short, all the attributes that ought to make them Eurosceptic. Yet, until very recently, criticism of the Brussels system was more or less confined to the United Kingdom and the Nordic world.

Not any more. When 62 per cent of Dutch voters rejected the European constitution in 2005, something changed. The peoples of the hither parts of Europe are rubbing their eyes and shaking off the enchantment. Not all of them, obviously. But it's striking that Dutch and Scandinavian Europhiles are starting to adopt the same defensive tone as their British counterparts.

All that is needed is a catalyst. European integration rests, to a far greater degree than its supporters like to admit, on a sense of inexorability. People might not have chosen political union but, since it is happening anyway, they shrug and go along with it. Euro-integrationists often use the metaphor of a bicycle: if the EU isn't moving forward, they say, it will topple over (a ravening shark that must keep swimming or drown might be a more apt image).

It is this fear that was behind the Euro-elites' determination to push ahead with treaty after treaty, despite the referendum results. The same angst lies behind their refusal to allow the stricken Mediterranean countries to leave the euro and start exporting their way back to growth.

If one of the four large member states were to secede, that sense of inevitability would evaporate. Other countries, too, would seek a free-trade-plus relationship in place of full membership. In time, they might join the four EFTA countries, Iceland, Norway, Switzerland and Liechtenstein, to form an outer Europe, linked to the federalist states through the broad nexus of a European free trade zone.

In effecting such a change, Britain might reasonably hope to improve her relations with Continental states. The EU was designed as a peace project; but as integration has become tighter, it is causing animosities among its peoples. By withdrawing from the argument, Britain would remove the single greatest cause of her quarrels with nearby lands. The core federalist countries would find, for their part, that they had lost a bad tenant and gained a good neighbour. Secession is now the greatest gift Britain could give Europe.

– Conclusion –

L et me conjure a cheerful vision for you. It's 2020, and the UK is flourishing outside of the EU. The rump Union, now a united bloc, continues its genteel decline, but Britain has become the most successful and competitive knowledge-based economy in the region. Our universities attract the world's brightest students. We lead the way in software, biotech, law, finance and the audio-visual sector. We have forged a distinctive foreign policy, allied to Europe, but giving due weight to the US, India and other common-law, Anglophone democracies.

More intangibly but no less significantly, we have recovered our self-belief. As Nicolas Sarkozy, President of the European Federation, crossly puts it: 'Britain has become Hong Kong to Europe's China.'

Part of our success rests on bilateral free-trade agreements with the rest of the world. The EU has to weigh the interests of Italian textile manufacturers, French filmmakers, Polish farmers. Even Germany likes to defend its analogue-era giants against American internet challengers such as Google, Amazon, Facebook and Uber.

Once outside the Common External Tariff, the UK

swiftly signed a slew of free-trade agreements, including with the US, India and Australia. Our policy is like Switzerland's: we match EU trade negotiators when convenient, but go further when Brussels is reluctant to liberalise, as with China. Following Switzerland, we forged overseas relationships while remaining full members of the EU's common market – covered by free movement of goods, services and capital.

Non-EU trade matters more than ever. Since 2010, every region in the world has experienced significant economic growth – except Europe. The prosperity of distant continents has spilled over into Britain. Our Atlantic ports, above all Glasgow and Liverpool, which were on the wrong side of the country when the EU's customs duties were imposed in the Seventies, are entering a second golden age.

London, too, is booming. Eurocrats never had much sympathy for financial services. As their regulations took effect – a financial transactions tax, a ban on short-selling, restrictions on clearing, a bonus cap, windfall levies, micro-regulation of funds – waves of young financiers brought their talents from Frankfurt, Paris and Milan to the City.

Other EU regulations, often little known, had caused enormous damage. The Reach Directive, limiting chemical products, imposed huge costs on manufacturers. The bans on vitamin supplements and herbal remedies had closed down many health shops. London's art market had been brutalised by EU rules on VAT and retrospective taxation. All these sectors have revived. So have older industries. Our farmers, freed from the CAP, are world-beating. Our fisheries are once again a great renewable resource. Disapplying the EU's rules on data management made Hoxton the global capital for software design. Scrapping EU rules on clinical trials allowed Britain to recover its place as a world leader in medical research.

Universities no longer waste their time on Kafkaesque EU grant applications. Now, they compete on quality, attracting talent from every continent and charging accordingly.

Immigration is keenly debated. Every year, Parliament votes on how many permits to make available for students, medical workers and refugees. Every would-be migrant can compete on an equal basis: the rules that privileged Europeans over Commonwealth citizens, often with family links to Britain, were dropped immediately after independence.

Britain has been able to tap into its huge reserves of shale gas and oil, which came on tap, almost providentially, just as North Sea gas was running out. At the same time, the free-trade deal with China has led to the import of cheap solar panels, which the EU had banned. They are now so integrated into buildings and vehicles that we barely notice them. Cheaper energy means lower production costs, more competitive exports and a boom all round.

Unsurprisingly, several other European states opted

for a similar deal. Some (Norway, Switzerland) came from the old European Free Trade Association; others (Sweden, Denmark) from the EU; yet others (Turkey, Georgia) from further afield. The United Kingdom leads a 21-state bloc that forms a common market with the EU 25, but remains outside their political structures. The EU 25, meanwhile, have pushed ahead with full integration, including a European army and police force and harmonised taxes, prompting Ireland and the Netherlands to announce referendums on whether to follow Britain.

Best of all, we have cast off the pessimism that infected us during our EU years, the sense that we were too small to make a difference. As we left, we shook our heads, looked about, and realised that we were the fifth largest economy on Earth, the fourth military power, a leading member of the G8, a permanent seat-holder on the UN Security Council, and home to the world's greatest city and most widely spoken language. We knew that we had plenty more to give.

Tom Kremer

AFTERWORD
– A Good European –

History is never an even flow. We learn it, and remember it, only by its highlights. There are moments of significance which cast their reach across centuries. Such an event, for example, was Chamberlain's return to the country in 1938 after visiting Hitler, waving a piece of paper high above his head, announcing the peace he has gained for all time to come. It is worthwhile recalling this particular incidence now because it has a disturbing similarity to the return of Cameron from his wide-ranging European excursions, with the same kind of paper, announcing the same message of a peaceful, permanent, living deal between the continent and our country, for all time to come.

Our prime minister has to be taken seriously just as Chamberlain must have been credited before the cataclysmic period that ensued. This is difficult enough, when Cameron's entire performance recalls a travelling salesman standing at your door, trying desperately to convince you to buy an item superior to anything you have seen in your life before. Cameron is now bestriding the country, full of victory boasts, claiming as a final, overwhelming fact that the victory he brought back was doubly good: good if the circumstances turn out to be favourable and good even if a dark climate envelops the whole continent. This is precisely the kind of promise anxious parents make to crying children when some specific action is required. The future does not really matter so long as the next few steps are taken.

We have to ask ourselves to what extent we are better or worse off by being members of the European Union. A systematic, relatively impartial study of this question was carried out by Open Europe recently. The conclusion reached by the study makes it quite clear that any advantage, one way or another, is minimal. In other words, any serious prediction of the economic outcome of the referendum demonstrates that the result will not make any significant difference.

Personally, I do not find the result of this research surprising. More than sixty years in commercial life has consistently shown me the underlying principle of commerce. In any transaction, when there are more sellers than buyers, the buyers benefit and when there are fewer sellers than buyers, the sellers have the advantage. If a Chinese official is in the market in search of a hundred and twenty planes, he will survey what is available and choose a make that is the best in quality and least expensive. It will be of no interest to him whether the plane is made in France, in the US or in Britain. He will spend not a single moment to consider the political affiliation of the plane's producer. It will certainly not enter his head to mull over whether Britain is, or is not, a member of the European Union.

What makes an economy dormant or vibrant depends on the cohesion, the talent, the freedom, the creativity and the ability of its society to harness these forces to produce what the world needs. These are the factors that help to determine the relative success of Germany, and also the relative paucity of the Southern states.

We know in great detail what the British resource has contributed in material substance to the life of humanity in the last three hundred years. The bridges, the rails, the factories, the cars, the naval vessels, the means of communication, the literature, all stand as convincing witness of our creative potential. There is no reason to suppose that any of this faculty would change whether we continue to be part of the European Union or return to our own wealthy resources.

There is one very significant sector of our economy that requires special treatment. The City of London is the world's leading centre of distinct financial transactions. In the course of the more recent past this position was occupied by Genoa, Venice, Switzerland, and Wall Street, all before the latest turn of fortune. The sequence of succession of these financial centres have many historical roots but the one over-riding factor they have in common is this one: they were all significantly independent of the powerful states to which they formally belonged. The banks operating from these centres managed, somehow or other, to be relatively free of the states' overarching authority in which they were embraced.

So, it is vital that we fully realise that any conceivable loss of political authority as a result of leaving the European Union will be more than compensated by the gains of the financial status of the city which provides more than 10 per cent of our economic life. And as personal fortunes grow and multiply the world over, from Russia, China, India and even Europe, the importance of London is likely to grow even further.

Apart from the banks and beyond the arid finances, there is the overall commercial scene that may alter as a result of a Brexit. This is a subject much cultivated by the forces who advocate the status quo. It seems that a perennial fear preoccupies a section of the population deeply worried about the loss of our membership of the European Union. Lord Rose, for example, 'chosen' to lead the NO-Brexit campaign, is forecasting a fearmongering financial loss if Britain leaves the EU and does not get a free trade agreement. He does not, of course, tell us exactly how and why this loss would occur. So we are asked to imagine various bods, both within and without Europe, who otherwise are sane and well experienced, deciding not to trade with us just because we are no longer members of the EU.

No matter how hard I try to conjure up such a scenario, I cannot think of any commercial organisation that would think like that. And the simple, and obvious, reason for such an impossibility is that in the real world if one has something to sell, the only thing that matters to him is to find a willing buyer. But let us assume that, for one reason or another, the European Union would wish to put obstacles in the way of such a deal. This is highly possible since the bureaucracy in charge of the Union has one simple, but overriding, principle: to preserve and enlarge itself. The status, the income, the pension, the security of tenure is inviolable.

But, fortunately in this instance, the trading pattern is in our favour. We are selling less to, and buying more from, our European partners. Thus any interruption or interference by the Union will hurt their members more seriously than Britain's.

Generally speaking, the currently unleashed debate assumes that whatever this country decides, in or out of the Union, the rest of Europe will continue to make its way eventually towards a single political entity: the ever more closely knit European Union. With half the unit doomed to borrow money, while the other half is condemned to lending the same money, it cannot become a permanent, long lasting single state.

*

It has become fashionable in some quarters, both here and on the Continent, to reproach the British for not being European enough. It is a curious reproach, especially in the mouth of leaders whose countries owe, in part, their independence to Britain. A good European is not easily defined. To aspire to this denomination, some integrationists believe, Britain should go with the Continental drift, with whatever the dominant political establishment in Europe has in mind. In that case, the British would have been better Europeans if they had let Napoleon have his way, or made peace with Hitler in 1940, or excluded the continent from the protective NATO umbrella. Perhaps this is why the only acknowledgement Britain has ever received for saving Europe from being a German continent, is an annual Christmas tree gifted by Norway. But then Norway is not, as it so happens, part of the European Union.

Perhaps being a good European means surrendering important national interests. For France this would amount to allowing the Common Agricultural Policy to be radically reformed and the relocation of the European Parliament from Strasbourg; for Spain, abandoning the claim to Gibralter and the right to fish around British coasts; for Ireland, Portugal and Greece, forgoing the benefits of regional subsidies, and so on. No major concessions of national interests seem to have been forthcoming from any EU members thus far. On the contrary, each and every European leader strives to protect and enhance the national interest of his own country and is judged by his constituency accordingly. David Cameron himself makes a great play on his commitment to defend British national interest above all else.

Then again, being a good European may translate into conformity to Brussels directives and compliance with EU rules. On such an official league table, France, unsurprisingly, is by far the worst offender whilst Britain comes somewhere in the middle. Unofficially, everyone knows that there are two ways of complying with European rules and regulations: the stricter way, as practised in Sweden, Denmark, Holland, Germany, Britain and Finland and the Mediterranean way. France is a special case, she continues as she has always done: she practices what is beneficial for her and disregards what is not.

If being a good European is measured by contributions made in respect of the rights and liberties of the individual citizen, the British must easily outrank all other nations. Religious, racial and political tolerance, freedom of speech, protection and equality in law, parliamentary democracy itself, were established here decades, if not centuries before they have come to be accepted as European ideals.

The debate about Britain's relationship with the Continent is bound to keep generating confusion of every conceivable kind. This debate should not be about Britain leaving the EU, about being anti-European, about exactly how far Europe extends, about the precise powers of a European president. The essence of this debate is about the kind of Britain people in this country want to have as their future home.

The motivation and drive towards integration

emanates from European political establishments. The unification of the continent is not inspired by the spontaneous yearning of its people. A future Federal European State is yet another grandiose vision dreamt up in the political culture and intellectual climate of a continent whose history is littered with the ruins of precisely such visions.

Having a currency, a written constitution, a parliament and a political president do not, in themselves, amount to an enduring political state. These trappings of power are not substitute for a single nation state living within well-defined boundaries. The magnificent achievements of what may be termed *European culture*, in the fields of Philosophy, Music, Law, Language, Literature, Art and Architecture, have their roots in individual societies with a sense of self-identity. To preserve the creative sources and cross-fertilisation of cultures it is vital not to merge the European nations into a standardised, politically homogenised state. A nation, a people, cannot be cobbled together in a matter of decades. The aftermath of Versailles and the post-colonial constructs in the third world should have taught us that much. This particular enterprise, without a strong, natural centre of power, will founder on the deeply ingrained national differences in character, culture, habit and attitude right across Europe. The political edifice presently under construction, in its ambition, scope and dimension, will render any kind of European Union ungovernable.

After all is said and done, the British people have a stark choice to make. They can do nothing and drift along with the Continental current or fight to preserve their eccentric, national identity. They can vote to remain in the EU, let control slip to Brussels and throw in their lot with a concentric majority. It is, in the short term, the easier option. It takes no effort, avoids confrontation, abrogates responsibility. To stand firm against a countervailing trend, to rely on one's own resources, to stick to principles, is much harder. It requires courage and self-belief. This is true of individuals as it is of nations.

On the Continent, decisions reached between political leaders at various summits are almost invariably endorsed or ratified by national parliaments with the general public left out of the equation. So the momentum builds and a new kind of political entity is being negotiated into existence in the artificial hothouses of international diplomacy without too many people being involved. This has ever been the way of life in concentric cultures, cultures that leave the ordinary man with a feeling that he has no say, that he does not matter, that he has no choice except to strike, to block roads, to mount barricades.

Thus far, politics in Britain has not worked like this. The independence of the country and the right of the people to be governed by consent, have been inviolate. Creeping continental integration poses a threat to both.

Cameron's troops are equipped and ready to launch the war. Nothing is likely to deter them from using every single means at their disposal to drown us in the deepest lake of fear imaginable. The people of this country will have to find their voice and make damn sure this voice is strong enough to command the attention of politicians tempted to negotiate, by subtle degrees, Britain off the map altogether. For what it's worth, I personally believe that the British will resist any further erosion of their decision-making powers. I believe that integrationist political leaders within all three parties, and the Brussels club, have seriously misjudged the mood of the country and the character of the people, something all too easily done in the frenzy of ongoing summitry. Political culture here is strongly based on non-conformism, on individual self-reliance, on grass roots democracy, on anti-authoritarian instinct, to be otherwise. If thirty-one small parish councils can combine on their own to effectively influence the traffic management of the A35, if a huge Countryside Alliance can spring up from nowhere, if government continues to live in fear of the popular press, then people of this country will surely not let go of their own identity. An easy-going environment, fluid and flexible structures, personal freedom and belief in the individual, are what made this nation great. If they have been helpful to the country in the past, these attributes are now critical for her survival.

If Britain is able to unite her people around the

anti-integrationist principle and adhere to it, she will be at the heart of the continent as the Greater Europe project falls apart. To lead in Europe it is not enough to be chummy with European leaders, to go with the mainstream, to be with the majority on this or that issue, to keep afloat in the tide of ever-changing alliances. To lead anywhere is to have firm principles and ideas and the strength to maintain them in the face of short lived trends. It is a quality of leadership that the British have manifested in abundance in the past.

British political and legal culture have deep roots. They have grown organically over centuries and have helped to produce a society in which the state and the individual are roughly in balance. An unprecedented degree of personal freedom and social rights are accommodated within the framework of a tolerated central authority. As the whole edifice is fully alive, with the social, economic, legal and political threads closely interwoven, externally inspired surgery on any one part affects the rest. There is something unique and precious about the civilisation of this country, perhaps not fully realised or appreciated by all its inhabitants. To tamper with it is reckless. To risk it is political folly. If, to be European enough is to harmonise British laws with those on the continent, to merge the country's institutions with theirs, to tailor local traditions to a continental norm, to castrate native political instincts, then, one sincerely hopes, Britain will never be European enough.

Then again it may be that to be a good European one should first of all be true to oneself. For how can any association of people or nations succeed if the members of the association, in the process, betray their own true identity? So the mission for Britain, with her proven European credentials, is today what it has been for centuries: to save the continent from the worst excesses of her visionary self.

On the Natural History of Destruction
by W. G. Sebald

In the last years of the Second World War, a million tonnes of bombs were dropped by the Allies on 131 German towns and cities. 600,000 civilians died. Sebald's classic essay explores the consequences for the German people, and his bafflement at German collective amnesia.

CLASSIC COLLECTION

The Classic Collection brings together the finest essayists of the past, introduced by contemporary writers.

Beautiful and Impossible Things
– Selected Essays of Oscar Wilde
Introduced by Gyles Brandreth

Words of Fire – Selected Essays of Ahad Ha'am
Introduced by Brian Klug

Essays on the Self – Selected Essays of Virginia Woolf
Introduced by Joanna Kavenna

All That is Worth Remembering
– Selected Essays of William Hazlitt
Introduced by Duncan Wu

*All NHE titles are available in the UK, and some titles are available in the rest of the world. For more information, please visit www.nottinghilleditions.com.

A selection of our titles are distributed in the US and Canada by New York Review Books. For more information on available titles, please visit www.nyrb.com.